Data Governance

PERSPECTIVES AND PRACTICES

Harkish Sen

Technics Publications
BASKING RIDGE, NEW JERSEY

TECHNICS PUBLICATIONS
TECHNOLOGY / LEADERSHIP

2 Lindsley Road, Basking Ridge, NJ 07920 USA
https://www.TechnicsPub.com

Cover design by Lorena Molinari
Edited by Lauren McCafferty

All rights reserved. No part of this book may be reproduced or transmitted in any form or by any means, electronic or mechanical, including photocopying, recording or by any information storage and retrieval system, without written permission from the publisher, except for the inclusion of brief quotations in a review.

The author and publisher have taken care in the preparation of this book, but make no expressed or implied warranty of any kind and assume no responsibility for errors or omissions. No liability is assumed for incidental or consequential damages in connection with or arising out of the use of the information or programs contained herein.

All trade and product names are trademarks, registered trademarks, or service marks of their respective companies and are the property of their respective holders and should be treated as such.

First Edition
First Printing 2019
Copyright © 2019 Harkish Sen

ISBN, print ed.	9781634624787
ISBN, Kindle ed.	9781634624794
ISBN, PDF ed.	9781634624817

Library of Congress Control Number: 2018966901

For M.S. – the one who has supported me every step of the way.

This is also dedicated to my family for their unconditional love and support.

Contents

Introduction 1
   Control and responsibility 2
   Data fitness 5

CHAPTER 1: Understanding Data Governance 11
   Is data governance just policy-making for data? 20
   Is data governance just data management? 21
   Communication is critical 23
   Data and accountability 25

CHAPTER 2: Owning Data Governance 27
   Technology and humans in society 28
   Law and data governance 32
   Personal identifiable information and data governance 38
   More data, more knowledge…more power? 42
   Data governance roles 45
   Data administrator 46
   Data protection officer 47
   Data steward 51
   Data architect 53
   Data procurement officer 54
   Data policy officer 56

CHAPTER 3: Data Governance Purpose 59
   What are the components within policy making? 60
   What do we mean by a data governance function? 62
   Setting the scene 63
   Moving from siloed behaviors to data for the organization . 64
   Clearly articulating the benefits 65
   Data confidence 69
   Data ethics 75

CHAPTER 4: Getting Data Fit 79
    Data governance using the 5-step method 80
    Step 1) a clear aspiration or high-level goal 81
    Step 2) developing principles from a clear strategy 82
    Step 3) testing the strategy 87
    Step 4) build out an operational plan for delivery 90
    Step 5) prototype different models and test thoroughly 93

CHAPTER 5: Data Governance Stakeholders 101
    Data policy 104
    Data analysis 105
    Data quality and maintenance 107
    Data technical management 109
    Data privacy and security 110
    Data Governance Scorecard 112
    Approaches, practices, and methodologies 116
    Agile vs. Waterfall 116
    Conducting thought showers in a bunker 121
    Getting your core assumptions in order 123
    Data governance business drivers 125
    Stakeholders understanding the importance of data 127
    Blockers as stakeholders 130
    Data governance questions 135
    About metadata 138
    About blockchain 139

CHAPTER 6: D474: A Case Study 141

Conclusion 191

Bibliography 197

Introduction

When we separate "data" and "governance," each word is universally understood. However, putting them back together creates a confusing multitude of approaches, definitions, and opinions. Once considered a technical data quality and management area, the term "data governance" has evolved into a myriad of different meanings and approaches. What makes data governance more challenging (and more vibrant) is the scope of coverage it has as a subject. One might consider data governance to be an umbrella term for many different technical, managerial, strategic, political, and legal data operations.

Data governance as a practice is growing exponentially. The boundaries of data governance are constantly expanding and the controls and monitoring protocols race to catch up. Navigating through the complexity and nuances of data governance need an appreciation of both theoretical and practical perspectives. This book will summarize a few of the more popular theoretical debates that are linked to data governance, such as the relationship between humans and technology.

Control and responsibility

Our data landscape has changed dramatically in recent times. Due to the advancements in technology, and the increasing power of data, the governance of data has found its way into greater public awareness. The advent of mobile technologies coupled with the ability to harness personalized identifiable information provides companies with greater insight into their customers and behaviors.

As data applications evolve alongside the demands for stricter data protection and greater transparency, the focus of data and its uses is now less operational and more political. We are now seeing a deeper and more complex role for data – one that requires the alignment of technology, communication, and people functions to ensure data is regulated and managed effectively.

Data governance has also become more prominent as a mechanism for exercising controls over online information gathering. Sure, it's no secret that companies' engineers have increased revenues by using customer information to create personalized online experiences. This is by no means a bad thing. Companies are more likely to invest in technologies that harvest customer information if they are proven to generate profits and gain an edge over other companies in hypercompetitive markets. The issue of gathering information across online and social media platforms – particularly gathering identifiable data – was recently brought to light over allegations into the misuse of personal profiling. Most recently, a UK-based company, Cambridge Analytica, was accused of using information from Facebook profiles to target and subsequently influence voting behavior. The ramifications are still to be established, but whatever they may be, this incident has proven how technology and data are now deeply embedded within society.

The Cambridge Analytica case revealed how the practice of personal profiling can be easily applied to other areas within society. In what might be considered "politically sensitive" areas, there are three separate issues around the use of profiling personalized data that come to mind:

1. **Profiling**. Firstly, the profiling of voters via online campaigning has surfaced and brought attention to a sensitive topic. By targeting specific demographic groups or identifying locations, one could argue that personal profiling could change the way future campaigning is conducted.[1]

2. **Fake news**. The use of "fake news" and less-than-objective news reporting algorithms could potentially create distrust between the public and mainstream broadcasting media. With potentially disruptive and provocative sources of information

---

[1] A Fresh Canvass: How online campaigning is influencing Britain's election; The Economist; https://econ.st/2ruataY (Accessed 28/05/18).

freely available online, it can be difficult to separate fact from fiction.

3. **Campaign meddling.** There are revelations of campaign meddling, both in the United States[2] and across the pond in the UK,[3] and some countries are taking extreme measures to prevent foreign powers from attempting to influence (or interfere) in their elections.[4]

Capturing global attention in this manner draws attention to the issues surrounding data governance. The controversies highlight the need to find and implement ways to prevent, control, and regulate the way we store and use personalized data.

The advent of stronger legislation, such as the EU General Data Protection Regulations (GDPR) with more punitive financial measures, may spur greater controls on how companies use personalized identifiable information. Indeed, GDPR may be the catalyst for further legislative measures guarding against what might be considered unethical data profiling practices.

---

[2] Senior Trump Advisor says Russian election meddling 'beyond dispute'; Gambino, L; The Guardian; https://bit.ly/2ELA87D (Accessed 25/06/18).

[3] Signs of Russian Meddling in Brexit Referendum; Kirkpatrick, D.D; The New York Times https://nyti.ms/2jsMpEV (Accessed 25/06/18).

[4] How Sweden is preparing for Russia to hack its election; Brattburg, E; & Maurer, T; Carnegie Endowment for World Peace & BBC; – https://bbc.in/2RKtl1b (Accessed 31/05/18).

Legislation and regulations are effective checks to help with compliance, but only if they are enforced properly and effectively. Naturally, the next question to ask is how diligent these new regulations will be audited by the relevant authorities. Can enforcement agencies keep track of all companies that are non-compliant? How will this compliance be monitored effectively?

Although the practicalities of GDPR enforcement are still in its infancy, the impact for organizations adopting stricter regulations are just as significant. The benefits will be even more obvious for organizations that currently have no measures in place to manage the fluid data governance landscape.

Data fitness

Many organizations continue to struggle with reaching consensus on basic operational definitions and interpretations, let alone how to take a holistic approach to data. Without clear governance practices in place, companies risk creating a vortex of data inefficiency, which will only hamper a company's ability to manage and use information effectively.

To meet the challenges of data governance, compliance, and future legislative change, organizations will need to ensure they are ready to adapt now. The size of the company is not necessarily an issue. Here, the approach and methodology will apply equally to both large organizations and micro-sized businesses.

Before refining or developing new data governance practices, however, an organization must first know where it currently stands in its own data fitness. The term "data fitness" describes whether a company is ready to handle data matters that could impact economic, operational, political, legislative, and technological aspects of the company. One way of doing this is to conduct a root and branch review of the organization to assess its data fitness.

Asking if a company is "data fit" means asking whether the organization has the right framework or data governance structures in place to ensure compliance. If so, is that data governance system robust enough to manage social, legal, political, and technical pressures effectively? Does the organization have effective controls in place to adapt to potentially increased regulation across its businesses? All of these factors are matters of data fitness. Tools to determine data fitness are set out in Chapter 4.

This is where creating a data governance program to support the business becomes essential. In some ways, data governance is about ensuring best practices continue to grow while encouraging new developments in data and technology.

This book contains six chapters:

- Chapter 1, Understanding Data Governance, looks at the broad definitions of data governance along with issues within data governance. We also consider the purpose of data governance and why its function is important to align strategy and operational practices. Effective data governance provides the needle and thread that binds things together holistically.

- Chapter 2, Owning Data Governance, looks at Ownership, Wider Perspectives, and Roles, and explores how transparent data governance can simplify the complexities of data ownership. Reviewing social and philosophical debates around technology helps to contextualize the importance of data. The objective is to provide a deeper insight into the active nature of data. As the demand for data-driven technologies continues to grow, it is important to understand how data governance can be aligned to provide effective controls. A specialist data function is needed to achieve these controls. The final section of this chapter looks at the various roles and responsibilities needed to succeed.

- Chapter 3, Data Confidence, explores using tools (e.g., standards, strategies, and policies) to clearly align business objectives with realistic IT deliverables and produce meaningful outcomes.

Having clear data governance embedded within the organizational processes will create a better environment to cultivate and grow confident data. Confident data ensures accuracy and quality, which helps the organization trust the information being produced.

- Chapter 4, Getting Data Fit, covers the basic elements required to make data governance work for your specific organization. There are five steps required to achieve a basic level of data fitness and effective governance.

- Chapter 5, Approach and Stakeholders, covers various ways to implement data governance to ensure there are clear milestones and trigger points for key stakeholders to approve each phase. A data scorecard is introduced as a tool to help guide an organization through the data governance process.

- Chapter 6, D474: A Case Study, concerns a fictitious company, D474, used to illustrate the various examples and scenarios for implementing data governance. As the book introduces several different concepts and ideas, D474 will be used to bring these themes together. The aim is to produce a case study of how a fictitious company like D474 might implement data governance in a practical sense. The main objective is to apply the most suitable elements from the case example to your own organization.

Practical data governance is very much a bespoke process. In other words, you pick the parts that work best for your organization and apply them accordingly. The point is, one size doesn't fit all here. In fact, managing a data governance system can be a delicate balancing act between existing and new practices.

Getting data governance right is not easy. It may not be a simple concept to grasp at first. But the hope is that this book will help you understand some of the perspectives and practicalities involved and work through the challenges of data governance.

CHAPTER 1

Understanding Data Governance

"Data governance? That's easy!" someone once said to me. "All you need to do is make sure people understand what it means." As I started to think about this in a deep and philosophical way, my thoughts were interrupted by my friend's further reflection: "What *does* data governance mean, exactly?"

In simple practical terms, governing data requires a common approach that runs through an organization to align strategy and operational practices together. Effectively, data governance is the needle and thread that sews things together. This chapter defines data and defines governance. We will explore a multitude of different perspectives.

Data governance can mean different things to different audiences. For example, senior business executives may equate data governance with data protection regulation, whereas IT practitioners may point to data quality and management. In effect, data governance is an ambiguous term.

A quick search of "data governance" on the Internet can leave you bewildered with the numerous definitions out there. Perhaps one way of understanding what data governance means is to break it down into its composite parts. The Oxford English Dictionary provides the following explanations for data: "facts and statistics collected together for reference or analysis" and "the quantities, characters, or symbols on which operations are performed by a computer, which may be stored and transmitted in the form of electrical signals and recorded on magnetic, optical, or mechanical recording media."[5]

The above provides a more technical explanation to data and this interpretation is more likely to resonate with those involved with solution-driven and physical layer systems. However, the Oxford English Dictionary provides another definition which suggests a broader philosophical meaning: *"Things known or assumed as facts, making the basis of reasoning or calculation."*[6] This takes a more abstract view and may be more appropriately paired with strategic or enterprise level perspectives.

---

[5] Oxford English Dictionary definition of Data https://bit.ly/2p0D9d2 (Accessed 18/02/18).

It is important to note that data is a fluid concept and therefore most definitions are likely to be broad in scope trying to capture some or most eventualities. Data is arguably the most frequently used term in Information Technology (IT). Yet like heterogeneous systems, data has numerous explanations, all of which hold valid descriptions of the truth.

If you are dealing with a technically-minded audience, language used at the physical or systems level is probably going to have more impact. Business stakeholders require plain English so it's probably best to keep it simple, providing concise explanations of technical terms when needed. So, if data is ambiguous and means different things depending on the audience, what about the term "governance"? The Oxford English Dictionary definition for governance is twofold:

- The action or manner of governing a state, organization, etc. For example, 'a more responsive system of governance will be required.'

- Rule; control. For example, 'I don't think he's a very nice guy; I would not like to live under his governance.'[6]

---

[6] Oxford English Dictionary definition of Governance https://bit.ly/2B3NxE8 (Accessed 18/02/18).

From my experience, the meaning of governance generally oscillates between both Oxford Dictionary definitions above describing control and action. Although the user may mean control and establishment of rules or policies for example, the intended recipient may well understand this to mean acting or changing behaviors in response to a situation or given subject.

There are competing approaches of governance that exist and are equally valid. The governance subject can be anything. But for this example, let's use an organization. An organization will use a set of rules that are likely to have been established by the executive board or by legislation of the City, State, or Country it operates within. In other words, the first definition of governance is *ensuring compliance with a broader set of rules*. It might be helpful to consider this as an organization looking upwards to conform to rules that have been established by legislation.

The tools used by the organization are likely to include policies, regulations, and standards. These tools are carefully drawn and set out to describe what is and what is not acceptable in terms of compliance with the rules. The regulation of these tools and monitoring against wider rules is a form of governance. This brings us to the second, yet equally valid definition of governance which can be defined as *using tools to monitor and identify gaps in compliance*. This could be described as a company looking across its parameters to ensure alignment with upwards compliance.

The rules themselves can be complex and difficult to understand, particularly if a new issue emerges that has not been addressed in legislation. Therefore, if a gap emerges between what is captured in the rules and what exists, then the organization will most likely look towards its practices (best or common) for an answer.

An organization's practices will usually be tools formed of common-sense approaches, previous behaviors, and perhaps most importantly, a defined set of guidelines that translate the rules into practical operational measures that ensure compliance.

So, if we have managed to identify non-compliant gaps in the organization, what are we going to do about it? Effectively, the organization will need to take some form of remedial action to become compliant again.

The third and final definition of governance is *taking remedial action to amend existing rules, standards, or practices to ensure any gap is closed*. This is best described as a company looking downwards or internally to address any potential deficiencies.

We have seen that there are a few competing but related definitions of governance. While some are focused on control, others are concentrated on action. What is the correct definition? Well, I think the answer lies somewhere in between. In simple terms, governance means *using a set of rules, tools, and practices to exercise control or action over a given subject.*

So back to the opening question, "What does data governance mean?" If "data" and "governance" are ambiguous terms, what happens if we put them back together? Reaching common agreement amongst experts on the meaning of data governance may take a considerable amount of time. However, Gwen Thomas's excellent article on data governance[7] summarizes the point by collating various definitions from several different perspectives: Data Governance from a business-driven perspective is *the execution and enforcement of authority over the management of data assets and the performance of data functions.* [8] The focus here is on management and performance of data assets and functions to deliver a service for the business.

A data governance function is responsible for delivering changes in the way that a company manages and exploits data and will be aligned to support the strategic vision of the business. For some organizations, the vision will be aligned to maximizing profits through greater efficiency.

---

[7] Defining Data Governance; Thomas, G; The Data Governance Institute; https://bit.ly/2zoKuYz (Accessed 18/07/18).

[8] What is Data Governance; Rouse, M; SearchDataManagement.com; https://bit.ly/2p1Q8bQ (Accessed 18/07/18).

For others, data governance functionality will mean tapping into information systems to better understand what their customers want and need. Harnessing this information into better analytical output, will help to generate better product development and ensure customer demands are being met in the right place and at the right time.

In contrast, the perspective from data administration is driven towards the management of data across the organization. Data governance in this context refers to the overall management of the availability, usability, integrity, and security of the data employed in an enterprise.[9] Here, we can see common IT terminology such as usability and data integrity to describe the actions needed to govern data effectively.

The definition of data governance is going to be abstract as it needs to have broad coverage. In my humble opinion, the practice of data governance means *"using a set of rules, tools and practices to exercise control or action over a given data asset."* Applying controls or taking a form of action, such as applying data standards to a dataset is an example of data governance. To recap, data, governance, and data governance have several different meanings depending on where you stand within the organization. While some areas of the organization require precision and greater

---

[9] The Data Stewardship Approach to Data Governance: Chapter 1; Steiner, R; Tdan.com; https://bit.ly/2zOC1MQ (Accessed 18/07/18).

accuracy, data governance can be applied for any specific purpose. However, it is important to make this purpose clear to all at the start to avoid any ambiguity across the organization.

As set out earlier in this chapter, data governance helps bring structure and coordination to handling data-related matters across the organization. Data governance, in other words, is the adhesive that binds together the strategic, policy, and operational elements. But just what does that look like? There are three main aspects of data governance:

1) **Accountability**. This is about ensuring there is better transparency in the way data is handled by the organization. In other words, there is clear ownership for every part of the data journey as it passes through and is used by the organization. Both management and operations must set clear and transparent parameters of ownership. Having clear accountability that runs through all levels of the organization is the first way data governance starts to bind the daily operational "as is" processes with the managerial and strategic "to be."

2) **Consistency**. A common approach increases efficiency and reduces siloed data practices across the business. Here, data governance is used to effectively remove inefficient processes across the organization. This can be a challenge

when faced with procedures that have become embedded within the culture of the organization. Obtaining a complete view of the business processes is helpful–in fact, it is essential. Once the current process view is obtained, the organization can start to question which processes are needed and which are not. This action helps to weed out inefficient practices and once these are established, data governance can start to consider standardized procedures. The benefit of creating a set of generic or general-purpose standards means that the same set of rules can apply across the organization. By ensuring the entire organization follows one set of rules, there is a greater chance of users handling data in the same way. By the same token, if users are following a set of agreed standards, this enables the organization to maneuver all its data assets to face the right way. The "right way" in this case is alignment with the organization's strategic ambition.

3) **Adaptability**. The flexible nature of data governance means that it can be embedded into existing practices without too much disruption. Once data governance has been implemented into daily practice, it can also quickly adapt its standards and tools to align with the strategic

ambitions of the organization by configuring data governance tools to replace legacy practices, silos, and local approaches, so that common procedures are used by all. If an organization has the strategic ambition to move its entire IT infrastructure to the cloud, data governance can help by creating standards that are cloud compliant in the current "as is" in preparation for the transition across to the new or "to be" state.

The application of the above core components helps to embed data governance into the "as is" and is more difficult to manage and maintain for the business. If there is no control from the center, there is an increased risk of siloed practices emerging across the organization. Siloed practices are limited in scope as they are often created to solve short term tactical issues for a specific business need. Removing siloed practices across the organization and introducing enterprise-wide standards and rules are critical in developing a common approach.

Is data governance just policy-making for data?

A policy helps to set out the issue, context, and recommended approach. It also provides decision-makers with a high-level overture of the issue and provides enough information to make an informed decision. There are many different approaches, but the most important factor is the ability to summarize complex issues using plain and simple language. Being able to capture issues in a way that people can understand is an essential part of communication. Policy tools are set out in later chapters.

So, is data governance just a form of policy making with data thrown for good measure? No. Data governance is a much broader subject matter that spans across several technology-focused areas. One might argue that you need a policy-making function for each subject matter area, such as data management policy, data acquisition policy, and data retention policy. Policy across all these data-related areas ensures that strategic thinking can be developed either separately or collectively.

Is data governance just data management?

Data management is about handling data according to existing processes or practice. It is about the adherence to existing rules that are in place to help support daily operations. The approach to data handling and exceptions is usually well-defined. Data governance isn't just about the day-to-day management of data, but also about future strategy and directing change in terms of processes and technology. Data governance effectively sets the overarching approach a company will take toward handling its data assets.

Good data governance is likely to bring wider transparency to business processes that normally remain hidden from the public eye. With the data governance spotlight shining brightly upon all aspects of operation, businesses are suddenly exposed in a way they may not be ready for. Some businesses may be ready to face the situation; others may not be quite so prepared.

Whether an organization is ready for data governance or not, senior level management might be surprised to find the discovery of inefficient processes. Probably of more concern would be the rediscovery of actions previously believed to be defunct but still live.

Why is the discovery of inefficient processes bad for business? Inevitably there are a few issues that cause concern for senior management. Duplicating actions that are not required causes time and resources to be wasted. If resources are being ineffectively utilized, there are likely to be costs involved. Linked to this unwanted expenditure is the revelation that management is now unable to identify areas of concern. If inefficiencies have been discovered in what management had considered to be "safe zones," then the question probably being asked across the boardroom is, "what other things are happening out there where we *can't* see?" Bringing data governance into an organization requires strategic and operational input to deliver the business changes needed. So how can we practically bring the strategic and operational closer together in to a more seamless process?

Communication is critical

Building better communication between both strategic and operational groups is critical. We know from a business process perspective, the relationship between policy and operations should be seamless. From the onset, the assumption has been that traditionally policy making incorporates blue sky thinking and strategic development.

On the flip side, we should see these strategic ideas become fully realized processes or systems as they are developed and implemented by the operational side of the business. Does the assumption of a seamless transition between both policy and operations hold true? The truth is more likely to be discovered when one of two scenarios occur. Firstly, a full-scale review of any particular system is conducted due to implementing changes or upgrades to the business. Secondly, an event has occurred that has caused the system to stop or malfunction creating significant concern to warrant further investigation. The two events are most likely to trigger a review of each step of a process.

Having conducted quite a number of product and process reviews, my personal view is there can be a tenuous relationship between policy and operations at times! Therefore, it could be considered an uneasy alliance in some instances. The cause is usually gaps in communication.

So why does a communication issue arise and how does this pose a potential issue between two areas that are fundamental to the business? There are several different reasons why communication fails within the business:

- Lack of communication cross-functionally. The risk of having colleagues 'heads down' focusing solely on their own work areas means any important messages across the business may not get through.

- Use of the wrong type of communication. If colleagues are using emails to communicate the importance of data governance, it doesn't help if you decide to use verbal conversation only.

- Lack of communication up and down the management chain. Perhaps, the most obvious reason listed yet remains so difficult for business to master.

Using data standards and data principles will ensure people understand the importance of using data. Equally, data policies on accountability will ensure that employees are aware of their legal responsibilities when handling data. Having a transparent approach to data as it passes through an organization is an effective way of handling a complex issue such as accountability. The next section will explore some of the complexities around data and accountability in more detail.

Data and accountability

As the demand for data-driven technologies continues to grow, so does the need for more accurate user information. It is important to understand how data governance can be used to provide effective controls.

The introduction of new technologies such as social media platforms have helped bring people together, albeit digitally. With legal controls now in place to help steer companies towards the ethical use of customer information, data governance is also being used as a practical tool to apply social controls. Small to mid-sized companies, large-scale organizations, and government agencies will have to comply with these data protection regulations and standards. It is this very need for compliance that brings us to the issue of accountability.

Accountability and data have not been the best of friends in recent times. The growing remit of data makes accountability harder to pin on individuals. In simpler times, accountability and data had a clearer relationship. It was easier to identify accountability because it would fall squarely within one role or business area. There has been a technological shift away from siloed data stores managed by one business area to centralized data stores that can be accessed by all. This means if all areas of the business have access to the same data store, it widens the risk of accountability.

From a practical perspective, it becomes challenging to apportion responsibility to any one area or individual. With the advent of improved services, particularly in the field of data technologies, more people than ever before are managing or controlling data. From a compliance perspective, this creates a challenge to identify any one given individual responsible, if there is a breach or error. From a granular level, there are of course, individual logons that can help clarify who was present when the breach occurred. Companies can usually cover regulatory requirements using a "click-wrap agreement" (by asking users to click and accept accountability) before using any company device.

CHAPTER 2

Owning Data Governance

Data ownership is effectively a question of the legal obligations and responsibilities over the control of information. Who does the data belong to? Does it belong to the originator of the data, or the entity which stores it? This is a question left to legal debate and conjecture but technologies are bringing the debate to a wider audience than before. There is a continuous shift in balance between technology advancements and data governance controls used to protect privacy. With the introduction of stronger legislation regarding the use of personal data, the balance has shifted towards applying controls on technological progress.

The introduction of the EU's GDPR has had a big impact on data practices across the largest of companies. [10] However, the size of the company is irrelevant here.

---

[10] New European Union Data Law GDPR Impacts are felt by largest companies: Google, Facebook; Denhart, C.A; Forbes; https://bit.ly/2E9Aggg (accessed 27/18/06).

Companies of all sizes that use personalized data must now obtain consent for the continuous use of customer information.

Let's consider the use of personal data and its nearly symbiotic relationship with social media. Some experts argue that social media is the biggest invention of our times. Whether that's a reasonable claim or not, the fact remains that today's society expects full integration with social media. Social media platforms are designed so people can upload and download the content of their lives in seconds. The resulting need for bigger and better platforms has spurred another evolutionary push in technology. With technology evolving exponentially, the "push" is more a case of the barn door being left wide open, without any measure of control! In some sense, this is a good problem to have. Challenging existing boundaries is the only way to ensure technology remains progressive, functional, and fit for its purpose.

Technology and humans in society

It is important to understand the wider debates around technology as these views also impact how data governance is implemented. Why? Data governance also falls under the umbrella of technology.

Authors such as Donald Mackenzie [11] emphasize the importance of social construction to technology. In this context, the term "social construction" is intended to mean that humans are responsible for shaping and driving technology forward, rather than the inverse. In other words, technology is developed through the different selection processes and decision-making patterns of human behavior.

Having interpretive flexibility is a fundamental human capability. The term relates to how opinions towards technology are created through the process of social and cultural interpretation. Humans, not technology, control the meaning and influence of technological advancement, not the other way around.

Another popular view is actor-network theory which takes a more controversial position on the issue. Actor-network theory suggests that humans and technology are actors playing equal roles within an interconnected network within society; actors are defined as entities within the network and the focus is on how they do things. Most important to actor-network theorists is the relationship between human actors and technology actors. In fact, there is no distinction made between human or non-human. Rather, the focus is how all actors interact together to achieve a common purpose.

---

[11] The social shaping of technology; Mackenzie, D; McGraw Hill Education / Open University; 2 edn (June 1, 1999).

Other authors such as Bruno Latour[12] and Michel Callon[13] argue that the interconnected network has evolved in such a way that humans are now dependent on technology. In other words, technology is shaping human development.

One more main tenet of actor-network theory is that people should stop being so fearful of the humanization of technology. Furthermore, humankind should welcome and readily accept these technological advances because they are created by humans, to serve or improve the quality of life for other humans. Developing this argument further, systems theory probes deeper into the relationship between entities. Here, this theory considers how all the parts work together as a greater collective or sum. Effectively this larger configuration of entities/parts working in unison towards a goal is more commonly known as a "system."

The main difference between actor-network and systems theories is the idea of reverse salience. A reverse salient is any component within a system that is less developed than other parts. Given the rest of the system cannot advance because a particular component is lagging (or worse still, working in an opposite trajectory), more emphasis is placed upon finding a solution. Given that a solution may

---

[12] Reassembling the social: An introduction to actor-network-theory, Latour, B; Oxford university press, 2005.

[13] Mapping the dynamics of science and technology: sociology of science in the real world; Callon, M; Law, J; Rip, A; Macmillan Press; 1986.

be beyond existing technologies, a more creative or innovative approach must be adopted.

In his book on networks of power, Thomas P Hughes cites arguably the most famous of reverse salience: the electric current. Hughes charts Thomas Edison's trials and tribulations during the development of direct current electricity and the testing of different battery configurations. Hughes focuses on Edison's efforts on direct current before the Nikola Tesla radical solution of alternating current flow. Often known as the War of the Currents,[14] the 1800s saw the emergence of two competing schools of thought: Edison promoting direct current and Tesla advocating alternating current. The point here is that both camps were pushing one another to develop more innovative ways to use electricity.

The approach was out of step with conventional thinking of the day, as technology was only available for 2-wired systems. As electricity was once considered radical, let's fast forward to the present and consider a similarly disruptive technology, artificial intelligence (AI).

Like the technology debate, AI is an emotive, multi-dimensional issue. There are pros and cons to both sides of the debate. Supporters of AI for example, will point towards robotics replacing humans in mundane, labor-intensive tasks, flight and surgical simulators, and perhaps

---

[14] https://bit.ly/2Ewdj7X (accessed 11/12/18).

most obvious that AI robots are able to carry out tasks without the need for regular breaks, food, and drink. Opponents of AI for example, are likely to focus on the following issues: the risk of creating unemployment for skilled workers if AI robots replace humans, if humans become too dependent upon technology there is a risk that human cognitive functions like intelligence and social awareness could diminish, and the biggest risk is that AI could potentially surpass humans as part of the evolution process.

Law and data governance

Data governance from a legal perspective, seeks to ensure all regulatory and compliance requirements are followed by all relevant parties. Although data protection and confidentiality rules vary from country to country, some basic data protection principles are usually applied. At the highest level these regulations govern the capture, use, and storage of personal information. Normally enacted by governments, legislation regarding data protection and privacy spell out exactly how companies, third parties, and government agencies may use individual data, with and without consent.

Data protection within Europe is generally considered to be the most regulated. For years, Europeans have waged legal and philosophical debates on balancing the rights of the state with the human right to privacy. With regards to privacy of individuals, arguably the most widely interpreted piece of European legislation is Article 8 of the European Convention on Human Rights.[15] This regulation is focused on human rights, rather than data protection itself.

Article 8 establishes the right to respect private and family life alongside correspondence. It is also explicit in that public authorities are not allowed to interfere with this right unless it is in the interests of national security, preventing crime, protecting health or morals, public safely, or economic well-being.

To interfere with the private rights of an individual, a state must meet three conditions:

1. prove that one or more of the above interests or protections are being abused or under threat,

2. interference in the privacy of an individual must be in accordance with the law, and

3. it is necessary within a democratic society to achieve these aims.

The United States, in contrast, has no one single umbrella legislation that covers the use of data collection,

---

[15] European Convention on Human Rights https://bit.ly/1foTq0D.

processing, and retention. Rather, there are several federal and regional (state) regulations that provide a framework for data privacy. One example is the Federal Trade Commission Act (15 U.S.C. §§41-58), which covers issues like unauthorized disclosure. The Financial Services Modernization Act Gramm-Leach-Bliley Act (GLB) (15 U.S.C. §§6801-6827) covers issues regarding the disclosure and sharing of information between financial institutions. However, it is worth noting that the sharing of personal identifiable information between third parties (such as financial institutions) is widely acceptable. The onus is on the private sector to self-regulate and ensure personal information is kept secure. There is also a separate provision aptly named the Health Insurance Portability and Accountability Act (HIPAA) (42 U.S.C. §1301) specifically for the regulation of medical data being shared within the wider health industry.

More recently, China introduced a cybersecurity law setting out parameters for governing information networks within its territorial boundaries. The legislation uses the term "Network Operators" to cover a whole array of subjects, including social media platforms, online shopping centers, and gaming sites. Essentially, any application that uses the internet is captured under the legislation. Data protection for the individual has also been considered. For example, individual consent is now required if a network provider uses personal information.

Article 43 of the Cybersecurity Law[16] gives any citizen the right to request that a network provider delete any personal data they currently have stored. However, at the time of writing, this cybersecurity legislation is only partially implemented; the full impact upon international network operators remains to be seen. Although there may be a greater emphasis on individual rights, it is worth noting that control remains firmly with the Chinese government. In contrast, the European Union is pushing for greater transparency. Its GDPR places greater accountability on data controllers and data processors.

Users of personal identifiable information will have to state their reasons for holding this type of data and for how long they plan to store it. The legislation is wide-reaching and applies to global companies that process personal data of EU citizens. According to the EU, "more than 90% of Europeans say they want the same data protection rights across the EU – and regardless of where their data is processed."[17]

Clearly, a greater understanding of the impacts of data usage is needed. To this end, a noteworthy effort has been produced by The World Economic Forum (WEF). The WEF commissioned a report to examine issues of trust in the context of personal data usage. Not surprisingly, responses

---

[16] https://bit.ly/2lrkfIQ.

[17] https://bit.ly/2QE9jIu.

from countries were diverse. Some of the variance between countries was due to cultural beliefs coupled with the willingness to handle technology and perceptions of government protection.[18]

Even with these variances, data collection and the control of information emerged as the two issues of most concern, followed by trust in the network operator. Interestingly, where data transactions equated to some form of benefit or "value exchange," this had more impact in China and India as opposed to views taken in European or North American countries. Again, this could come down to different cultural values as mentioned above. More detailed work is required to better understand the nuances of differing legislation and how it impacts those affected.

Jamie Carter provides a helpful summary of data privacy laws across the world.[19] Carter argues that although there is a lack of centralized data privacy standards in countries beyond the Atlantic, the world is still in flux. In other words, global harmonization of data privacy laws is still a long way off. So, some countries have stricter data protection, other jurisdictions do not. Is this because people in countries that have lax data protection laws place their faith in government to safeguard and regulate?

---

[18] https://bit.ly/2G3u3oD (accessed August 2017).

[19] Beyond the Atlantic: Data privacy laws around the world; Carter, J.; Techradar.Com https://bit.ly/2PuoCyR (accessed 26/06/18).

Or is the issue clearer cut in that people now accept governments will hold personal information on all their citizens?

Richard Farkas in his blog asks the more direct question "Who cares about data privacy?"[20] Summarizing global research conducted by ComRes, a UK company, Farkas makes the point that the answer is complex and can be associated with cultural values. For example, individuals in countries such as the US generally take responsibility for their own data protection, whereas attitudes in countries such as Germany tend to trust that data privacy rules will be enforced by the government.

However, there is something inherently stereotypical and potentially troublesome to continue down the path of sweeping generalization. Just because some trends indicate a behavioral preference over another, does it really mean a whole country can be labeled with that attitude or type? This potentially creates a sense of unconscious bias. It also plays to possibly outdated views or beliefs. But ironically, perhaps the only way to break these stereotypes is to continue more research, to develop more informed perspectives.

---

[20] Who cares about privacy? Surprising facts from the globe; Farkas, R.; Argonaut Online https://bit.ly/2PoT25q (accessed 26/06/18).

Personal identifiable information and data governance

From the perspective of government, one could make the case that it is imperative to hold only basic information on citizens, even if only to protect and defend the rights of its nationals. However, considering increasing security threats and terrorist attacks on a global scale, there has been a shifting position for governments to acquire more personal identifiable information (PII).

From a technical or master data management (MDM) perspective, the most effective way to ensure accurate and effective data capture is by creating unique identifiers for each single entity. An entity, in practical terms, is one unit that cannot be broken down any further. Taking the scenario for governments to gather more accurate information on citizens, MDM experts using current technology would advocate the introduction of a national ID system to ensure a master record for everyone.

Several countries have introduced systems allowing their governments to capture information on how citizens interact with welfare and social services. For example, welfare areas such as housing, health, banking, and taxation will touch most of society; it is important to understand how citizens engage with these areas of government. Capturing data on specific transactions across each sector will help governments understand how to build better policy in the future. For example, Sweden has introduced the Nationellt Identitetskort (National Identity Card), which can be used to prove biometric identity and grant access to various government services. Applying for an ID card via the Skatteverket (Swedish Tax Authority) also entitles the user to receive an e-ID, which can used to verify identity in transactions with banks, public authorities, and Swedish companies.[21]

In addition to Sweden, India has introduced a national identifier called the Aadhaar card. Under the auspices of the Unique Identification Agency of India, a card was created with the objective to issue unique identification numbers to all residents of India that is (a) robust enough to eliminate duplicate and fake identities, and (b) can be verified and authenticated in an easy, cost-effective way.[22]

Since issuing the first Aadhaar card in September 2010, there have been nearly 120 million ID cards issued to Indian residents; this number continues to rise.[23] The Aadhaar card is becoming an increasingly valuable and important tool for identity verification. For example, the Aadhaar card is now linked to accessing government

---

[21] Electronic identification with the ID card; Skatteverket; https://bit.ly/2El8dqO (Accessed 25/03/2018).

[22] About UIDAI (Unique Identification Agency of India) https://bit.ly/2EiUuoZ (Accessed 25/03/18).

[23] Ibid.

subsidies including pension funds, Liquefied Petroleum Gas discounts, and financial investments. The use of the Aadhaar card has also been instrumental in deterring the practice of fraudulent voting. Since March 2015, the Indian Government decided to link voter ID cards to the Aadhaar card to curb multiple votes by any one individual. As a result, voter registration now requires the user to present both Aadhaar and Voter cards in the presence of an official.

Adopting such a large-scale biometric program across India has had more than the typical implementation or MDM challenges. These challenges usually relate to the process of creating a single source of master record.

Once a unique identifier has been established, in this case an employee ID number, it becomes the first step to mastering data effectively. However, establishing a unique identifier isn't the only technical challenge – establishing the data model, defining the business rules, and accessing security protocols are all issues that need to be considered. Imagine the scale and magnitude of implementing MDM for a country that also happens to be the world's largest democracy!

Other essential services like opening a bank account or purchasing a mobile phone require an Aadhaar card. In the aftermath of recent terrorist attacks where funding and mobile communications have been used to a devastating and deadly effect (most notably in Mumbai in 2008), the

Aadhaar card is now being used by the Indian Government as an additional security measure.

The implementation of the Aadhaar card has not been without its concerns. From a data privacy perspective, the widespread use of the Aadhaar card could be viewed as functional scope-creep, given that its original purpose was to validate identity to access public services. Functional scope-creep in this sense means a product going beyond the scope of its intended purpose. What was originally intended for ID verification is now being used differently as a functional tool for national security.

Although security measures might be justified in one way, the political question is whether it is the right approach. Legislating for one purpose but using it for another purpose has repercussions in that it sets an unwelcome precedent. For example, in the future would the dual nature of such a product be made transparent to the public at the time? If not, the repercussions are that the public may have been duped into accepting a product without being fully aware of the implications or consequences.

Those opposed to using such widespread digital identification would seriously question the amount of information being held by the state. Is it fair and proportionate in a democratic society? Is the state infringing upon fundamental human rights? What about the continued risk of personal profiling and its usage to influence behaviors beyond marketing or consumer choice? One thing is certain; the philosophical question of human rights and freedoms, contrasted against government control of personal data, continues to be an emotive topic.

More data, more knowledge…more power?

This section looks at how the analysis of data has become integral to many sectors of society. With the desire for more information increasing and technology capability of delivering this at greater speeds, data is now one of the key determinants to gaining a competitive advantage in the marketplace. The use of data is now commonplace, but there is a risk developing in earnest. This section will also look at how the threat of using collected data for unintended purposes continues to play out in the background. Is the thirst for data in this context, a strategy to acquire power, or a ploy to disrupt?

The traditional adage of *knowledge is power*[24] is appropriate in this context. Gathering and analyzing data at rapid speed is becoming increasingly important. We have seen

---

[24] The original quotation is derived from Sir Francis Bacon: Nam et ipsa scientiest [knowledge itself is power] from "De Haeresibus" [Of Heresies] in his Meditationes Sacrae [Sacred Meditations] in (1597).

computers and automation/robotics replace repetitive manual labor on the factory line, for example. We now use artificial intelligence technology to create machines that can self-learn. Machines perform greater analytical tasks, like processing website cookie information to enable better understanding of customer behavior.

The identification of such trends and patterns has become essential to success in a wide array of sectors. One industry which has benefited immensely from the use of big data, is sports. Jonathan Sullivan, in his insightful article on mathematics and football,[25] charts the evolution of data analysis in football.

Although it has become commonplace for football teams to scout new talent based on player performance statistics and averages, this important data gathering activity had its origins in a different sport altogether. Applying data science to analyze player performances grew popular in the sport of baseball. Billy Beane and the Oakland Raiders are known for using sabermetrics, which was (at its time) a pioneering, evidence-based approach designed to filter out performance statistics across several key areas, including running, fielding, and batting averages. The Oakland Raiders' use of data analysis to scout and recruit specific talent was popularized into a bestseller book (written by Michael Lewis, 2003) and a Hollywood movie (directed by

---

[25] Mathematics and Football; Sullivan, J; BBC; https://bbc.in/2PsJO8j. (Accessed August 2017).

Bennett Miller, 2011), both entitled *Moneyball*. Today, the use of statistical information is generally considered to be a core feature for teams looking to buy new players. The higher their statistics, the more valuable players become.

The point here is that data is now more readily available than ever before, even personal data. Given the movement towards greater transparency, the question arises: who becomes responsible for a data breach or infringement? Within a business, the likely answer is the most senior person within the company.

In the world of data, this is where accountability becomes a challenging area to navigate. Data may be handled by many individuals, or even an entire organization, in any one transaction. How is a company supposed to implement a system that can be both equitable and effective in managing data infringements on such a scale? For an example, we can turn to the recent allegations regarding the UK data analytics company Cambridge Analytica accessing Facebook profiles without user permission to gain voting leverage. Clearly, the moral of this story is that independent data governance is needed to ensure misuse of power does not arise.

From a technology platform perspective, perhaps this is a sign of the times; maybe traditional electoral canvassing is becoming somewhat outdated. Reaching the voting individual is best done directly through their devices. While there are obvious business cost benefits to moving things online, handing personal data over to a third party is done so at some risk. Without proper controls or permissions, companies are able to use data for other purposes besides market research.

As we have seen with the Cambridge Analytica example, this is where it is essential to establish a clear framework of data governance that sets out and enforces the rules for dealing with such a breach. For instance, if a dataset is owned by different business areas, each data owner will have to take responsibility. Business rules captured within a corporate governance framework should also describe the procedures for dealing with inappropriate conduct.

With size of company being an issue, one person may need to take overall responsibility. The smaller the company, the more likely one person will have a greater remit of responsibility. For example, the position of IT Director in a smaller company is likely to cover all IT areas including data, whereas larger companies are likely to separate out data and IT roles.

Data governance roles

Your company may have a senior position such as a Chief Data Director (or a similar title) in place who carries the strategic accountability for guiding, implementing, and enforcing a data governance system. However, the role of Chief Data Director is not always focused on technical outputs. The full immersion and permeability of data across an organization demands a strategic and business-orientated approach.

Below the senior level, a multitude of data roles exist across organizations. Depending on the size of the company, these roles are either narrowly defined but deep in terms of scope and remit, or widely encompassing but high-level. Naturally, this list is not all-encompassing; roles are crafted by different types of businesses with diverse needs. Here we will discuss some of the most common roles within a data-driven environment.

Data administrator

A data administrator is responsible for data entry input, updates, and integrity of database systems. Historically, the role was called a "database administrator". Advancements in technology have caused a gradual shift away from buying hardware database servers to leasing storage facilities on the cloud. There are many reasons for this transition to cloud-based technology, but the two most popular reasons are cost and space efficiency. The costs associated with maintenance and potential upgrades to hardware are removed; this becomes the responsibility of the owners of the cloud. With regards to physical space, the company no longer needs additional warehousing or floor capacity to house large servers or databases; again, the owners of the cloud are the ones who must contend with this issue. It hasn't taken long for companies to catch on to the economic benefits of using the cloud, along with greater reliability and enhanced security.

Data protection officer

This role has emerged from the EU GDPR as a mandatory requirement for both the private and public sector. Granted, it may not be applicable to countries that operate outside Europe. However, with information sharing increasingly globalized, it may be sooner rather than later when larger, non-EU companies are impacted by GDPR regulations. Within GDPR, however, there are some caveats to the role of data protection officer in relation to frequency and volume. For example, a data protection officer is accountable to ensure, firstly that the core activity of data usage is the regular processing and systematic monitoring of data subjects and secondly, that the frequency of data usage is happening on a large scale. The definition of large scale is somewhat abstract but there is a correlation between company size and composition. The larger the company, the more likely the requirement to have a data protection officer posting.

In terms of role and responsibilities, Article 39 of the GDPR provides some direction on scope. Officers, for example, should monitor GDPR compliance through internal audits and impact assessments. The focus of an internal audit is to ensure that effective controls and governance are in place to manage risks across the organization. The audit itself tests the robustness of risk management processes and serves as an assurance function to the executive board.

An impact assessment is a performance measurement tool designed to help quantify the ratio of extent of change to operational practices or processes. However, from a data perspective, an impact assessment is likely to be required when processing high volumes of personal identifiable information or using new technologies to share or hold sensitive data.

As part of the data governance process, the impact assessment should include:

- A clear description of the security and risk mitigation measures in place. Setting out these processes will help demonstrate compliance when dealing with personal level information;

- An outline of the business rationale for large dataset usage. This enables the company to show its use of personal data, although potentially high in volume, is proportionate and effectively managed; and

- A summary of the business operation/process of data usage and demonstrating the potential risk to individuals and how this is mitigated by meeting legal obligations for protecting large volumes of personal data throughout.

The data protection officer should also act as the company's representative and initial contact point for any data-processing activity. As a newly established data protection function, the initial contact with internal or external parties is extremely important. Why? In short, that contact is the public face of the business in relation to data.

Another important function of the data protection officer is to provide training and guidance to employees regarding individual obligations and responsibilities when handling data, particularly training the need to protect individual rights and freedoms.

The role of data within an organization has never been as important. There is a twofold reason I would like to offer up to explain the phenomenon. Firstly, the realization of data as a strategic asset has risen upwards dramatically. Some might say that technological capability in harvesting the potential of data has breathed new life into companies. Being able to use data in a way that reaches your customers and beyond is a beneficial asset. Secondly, the exponential rise of data has brought it to the center of attention. We now have media campaigns such as Experian recently promoting individual credit reports as one's data self. The credit report allows financial institutions to assess your suitability to borrow money.

The higher your credit score, the more likely you'll be accepted for credit applications.[26] The marketing strategy of linking personal reports of historical finances to a self-portrait of data is not only clever but also raises wider awareness of data in the public domain.

The right to be forgotten is also enshrined within GDPR legislation. The processing of data becomes relevant when large amounts of personal information is captured and stored for different purposes (for example to use in profiling, healthcare, or legal proceedings). The GDPR also places emphasis upon company training and guidance to ensure large companies and their employees are aware of the legal obligations towards protection of data.

The numerous and diverse duties of the Data Protection Officer place a lot of responsibility and accountability on this one individual. The Data Protection Officer must be acutely aware of GDPR rules, as a breach of the GDPR can result in punitive measures. The penalties can range from up to €20m Euros or 4% of the company annual global revenue, whichever is greater.

As with existing data protection legislation in the UK and parts of Europe, a Data Protection Officer can be held personally liable for a security breach of individual-level data. Any breach must be reported to the relevant

---

[26] "Data self-cramping your style?" https://bit.ly/1jN26x5 (Accessed 28 December 2017.).

authorities and individuals within 72 hours, unless the breach is of low risk to the rights of the citizen or group concerned.

Data steward

Of all the roles listed, this is probably the position that best encapsulates the principles of data governance. Fundamentally it is about having clear controls in place for the end-to-end management of data. The data steward is the data governance representative in the field and must understand all levels of the business.

Arguably, the biggest challenge for data stewards is understanding remit. Because data flows across all parts of the organization, one person alone cannot be expected to know every single process or take responsibility for the whole. This is where the data steward would be expected to demonstrate collaborative communication with other data architects, policy makers, and business personnel to ensure the data flow is properly monitored and captured across the organization. Data stewards must also show an ability to exercise diplomacy and build relationships with others. This is an understated but critical skill to the role. This is because data is permeable across all functions of the business; each area may take ownership of the data as it passes or flows through. A good data steward ensures that all areas understand the centralized controls and processes for data governance. The data steward will be embedded in all areas of the business, acting as a public relations specialist for any matters related to data. The data steward must be able to communicate in both the language of business processes and the language of technology, to identify and resolve data issues as they arise, in three important layers.

Often referred to as three-layer architecture, the first layer is presentational and describes customer interaction with the application. It is usually placed at the top, because this is where interaction between the customer and the organization first occurs. Also described as a digital platform in architectural terms, this is where online websites are often hosted and where the first entry point for data passing between the customer and organization occurs.

The second layer is often known as the logical tier. Being logical, this layer sits in the middle, acting as the conduit between both the presentation (upper) and the data (lower) tiers. The logical layer contains applications that integrate and coordinate functions including calculations, decisions, queries, and moving data between all tiers. The logic layer will request the information from the data layer, evaluate it, and process it, before passing it back up to the presentation layer.

The third layer is known as the data layer. This layer is responsible for storage and retrieval of information. The data layer may be a physical repository, an enterprise data lake, or based in the cloud. The data steward must be able to understand lower-level technical specifications of data flow across the system. Further, it is essential for data stewards to also understand data flow at the enterprise level. Stewards may work with business analysts to capture business requirements alongside current processes and ensure compliance with existing regulation.

The key role of a data steward is to ensure that any data passing within their remit is being used in accordance with the rules and regulations of the business. The data steward would be expected to use tools such as data standards to promote best practices, and to lead by example in demonstrating the correct use of data.

Given the vast scope of tasks covered by the data steward, a business may wish to split up the role to ensure that all areas are managed effectively.

Data architect

A data architect could be defined quite simply as a person who is passionate about all things data! Like their counterparts in construction, the architect will be tasked with designing technical plans for a construction of data. Most likely to be involved in the oversight of build and development, the data architect will be involved in the capture and design of data models. These data models will be capturing different levels of interaction across the organization.

First, the enterprise or conceptual data model will look at processes at the highest, overarching level. This is to help the business understand current processes. Next the logical data model will dig several layers deeper to evaluate the logical transactions between systems and see how data is transmitted.

Other duties of the data architect include producing artifacts as part of an application architecture system design. These include use-case diagrams, distribution/migration diagrams, matrices related to all levels of technology, and communications diagrams.

We have seen the role of the architect develop in many ways. From the technical specialist there has been a dynamic shift towards a business consultancy role. This role requires tact, diplomacy, strategy, vision, and a lot of patience!

Data procurement officer

The position of data procurement may not be featured in smaller companies since many activities may be covered under one general role. Data procurement, indeed, is a form of governance. Acquiring new datasets requires the company to be in a position to accept and use the information acquired. Although this may appear to be a straightforward concept, at a technical level there might be issues with the actual transfer of data. For example, the data character and field length sets might be incompatible with the company's data standards, so the procurement officer will have to bring in the data steward and data architect to ensure a swift resolution. In this case, the steward would record the gap in company standards and work with the architect to either modify the acquired dataset or the data standards, whichever is more practical. Once the technical issues have been resolved, the matter is then returned to the data procurement officer to resume acquisition. The data procurement role also requires an understanding of business processes, analytics, and reporting, for the company to harness all the benefits of the newly acquired data.

As the importance of data becomes more valuable to businesses, information of better quality is also being recognized as a vital commodity. In some cases, companies may not have all the information they need within their own environment. A company may have basic information on customers such as name and address, but lack any datasets on financial history. Many businesses want to know in advance whether customers have good or bad financial history. Acquiring data on customer activity (e.g., previous defaults, bankruptcy, and changes to financial credit scores) may help companies to better manage their risk portfolios. Experian[27] is one example among many companies that provide such services. The more information a company has available, the better informed its decision-making is likely to be.

The role of a data procurement officer is to manage the acquisition of new data services, bringing them into the organization aligned with existing data standards and security protocols. The commercial negotiations may be handled by the corporate finance team, but the data procurement officer should be involved in discussions related to technical capability, format, and transformation of data.

Data policy officer

The important role of a data policy officer requires the post holder to be fluent in technical, project management, and business-driven language, possessing the ability to communicate and ensure the message is understood across the business. The data policy officer will look to implement new regulations or processes that help improve efficiency or ensure an organization remains compliant.

Quite often the main concern for policymakers is to ensure the data policy in question can stand up to scrutiny. A policy must be able to adapt to changing circumstances

---

[27] https://bit.ly/2G2cGoi accessed 10/02/2018.

and work in any given scenario. This assumes that policymakers would have conducted risk assessments to test the robustness of the data policy.

Role	Function
Data Administration	Responsible for data entry input, updates, and integrity of database systems.
Data Architecture	Designing technical plans for a construction of data. Most likely to be involved in the oversight of build and development. Also involved in the capture and design of data models.
Data Policy	Implementing new regulations or processes that help improve efficiency or ensure an organization remains compliant.
Data Protection	Acting as company representative and initial contact point for any data-processing activity. Also provide training and guidance to employees regarding individual obligations and responsibilities when handling data, particularly training the need to protect individual rights and freedoms.
Data Procurement	Managing the acquisition of new information into the organization. Also requires an understanding of business processes, analytics, and reporting, for the company to harness all the benefits of the newly acquired data.
Data Steward	Acts as the data governance representative in the field and must understand all levels of the business. Usually embedded in all areas of the business, acting as a public relations specialist for any matters related to data.

Having considered some of the wider perspective and roles around data governance, we now turn towards the practical approaches. The following chapters look at the purpose, different techniques, and approaches required to build an effective data governance system.

CHAPTER 3

Data Governance Purpose

At the midway point of this book, it's worth returning to an important question that was raised earlier. Is data governance *really* just policy-making for data? The conclusion was no. In fact, data policy requires a detailed level of technical understanding that might not be available to the mainstream policy area within a business. However, the approach to data policy is based on the same principles that apply to a mainstream policy function.

Let's look at the components required for policy making and the potential definitions for data governance.

When first setting out on the data governance journey, one of the first challenges is whether it can be absorbed into an existing business function. If data governance were to be mapped across to an existing business function, the most likely destination would be policy-making. Most organizations have a policy making function, so wouldn't data governance just be an extension of policy focused on data-related matter, or is this an over-simplification of a more complex issue?

What are the components within policy making?

The machinations of government require effective policy making ability to meet the needs of departments, senior officials, and ministers. To deliver effective policy requires several components to be working in harmony. This may include:

- Review/Idea generation – having an idea that could improve an existing process or policy.
- Testing – creating a positive and safe environment to test for robustness.
- Senior sponsorship – to support and encourage sign-off at executive board and ministerial level.
- Awareness – using policy tools (briefings, papers, draft bills, public consultation documents, etc.) to raise wider engagement across key stakeholders and seek agreement to formalize idea into an initiative.
- Delivery – roll out new initiatives against clear milestones.
- Evaluation and review – reflect on how an initiative is working and seek improvement.

Idea generation is about making a preliminary journey into identifying potential pitfalls and remedies at an extremely high level. Compiling all these issues and mapping out the cost benefits for each potential solution normally results in a clear recommendation for the business.

Based on the proposed recommendation being endorsed and signed off by the appropriate management or governance, the next two steps of design and scope usually flow together. In other words, scoping will normally be looking at a more detailed understanding of the as is system.

Seamlessly interchangeable with scoping, the design phase will build upon the current system specifically looking at how best to align essential business requirements through tweaks, changes, or upgrades to create a new system.

Implementation is about putting the system into practice. Normally this is done with a smaller group to test and evaluate any teething issues. The results of the user group will help decide whether it is safe to roll out the system on an industrial scale. Widening the scope of rollout also requires managing the organization through this process by providing publication, guidance, and marketing material to help support the change.

Testing systems involve developing the technical requirements needed for the new system. From an architectural perspective, this means moving down the levels of granularity to look at specific components, coding, and testing these under different environments.

Finally, the last step in the process is evaluation. Because the pace of change is set at such a frantic pace, organizations often feel compelled to stay ahead with the latest available technology. With that said, evaluation is an important step in understanding whether any project is successful. The lessons learned are a critical factor in helping new projects with similar requirements being planned more effectively.

Looking at this issue more closely, one can start to make assumptions about the nature of the relationship between policy and operations. The current structure shows an indirect relationship between both groups and this is via the business only. It is hard to know the exact frequency of contact, but it is most likely infrequent or non-existent.

What do we mean by a data governance function?

The remit of data governance is wide-ranging. It is important that governance and policies are sufficiently robust to realize the strategic vision of transformation into a richer data-driven organization. From a data governance perspective, the purpose of data policy is to strategically inform the governance, acquisition, ingestion, transformation, and analytical use of information which is under the control of the business. The impact of data means data governance will be a key driver across the business, working with key stakeholders to develop data policy that is aligned to strategic business priorities and senior management commitments.

There is a close interdependency between policy and strategy. However, the key objective is for data governance to establish a clear set of data controls, guidelines, and rules that are underpinned by policies that champion all data as an asset for the business.

Setting the scene: How can data governance influence business strategy?

The data governance function is dependent on key stakeholders across the business driving the strategic vision forward. Key stakeholders include: lines of business, the IT team, and the Finance and Executive Board. Data governance can work with lines of business through the policymakers at the conceptual stage of policy design. The benefits of this approach are to embed the principle that data is a strategic asset of value and clearly understand what outcomes are achievable within expected timelines.

Moving from siloed behaviors to data for the organization

Moving from silo-orientated behaviors to an organizational-driven approach is a key priority for business transformation. Within organizations, there may already be established working relationships between business areas across several areas, including the coordination of Data Standards, third party information, and sharing information with other companies.

Through ownership of data standards, the data governance team will have an important strategic role in ensuring transformative programs embed the common standard for data approach across the business.

The IT department as a provider of technical solutions is another key stakeholder in ensuring the organization can benefit from cleaner and richer data. Through transformation, the data governance would work collaboratively with the IT department to ensure that data standards and any enterprise applications are mapped for future technical solutions.

The Data Quality Service will flag data quality across legacy systems and handle data inconsistencies as soon as they arise. A tactical solution might be to cleanse (or scrub) the data. Depending on the degree of issue, such as incorrect formatting, type, or character length, the service will look to resolve or escalate upwards to the data governance board for a steer or decision. Any issues arising from efforts to map out the end to end processes will also be escalated to the Data Governance Board, which will act as the final decision-making authority on issues of contentious or sensitive nature.

Clearly articulating the benefits of having richer data across the business

The benefits of richer data include an improvement in data quality, the ability to have greater confidence in the use of data for compliance and risk activity, and the capacity to analyze larger scale datasets across a broader range of variables. Messages to communicate include:

- *driving up quality across the business through focused data quality interventions (DQIs)* which are two-fold: 1) tactically in the short term, work collaboratively with the business to cleanse target areas and 2) strategically longer term, look at solutioning options with key stakeholders (including IT, Finance, lines of business, and senior executives);

- *turning data in to a strategic asset to benefit the business* is no longer data ownership by a particular function, but data for all of the organization;

- *joining up with existing program management activity*, for example, ensuring any information capture being devised is aligned to overarching data standards;

- *providing informed policy-making for the business* by building assurance and quality into the process of data acquisition and exploitation, policymakers will be able to rely on a more sophisticated approach to policy development through better predictive analytical capability;

- *building a stronger reputation across industry by sharing data* and working closely with policy and legal areas of the business to ensure that any disclosure of information is proportionate, legally possible, and provides strategic value to our wider customers across the industry;

- *providing integrity assurance and enforcement through clear data governance and accountability across the business, using* the data standards as a template and working with the business to build risk management controls upon the data received, stored, transformed, and utilized;

- *producing clearer governance and accountability* around data users and data ownership, by collaborating closely with the legal team to ensure any new data legislation is followed in a practical and compliance sense;

- *mitigating strategic risks by exploiting data in more effective ways*, such as leveraging data acquisition to better understand storage technologies to help the business make informed decisions on the risks around data prioritization, storage, and access for predictive analytical use;

- *informing policy change through data quality*, by ensuring all external information coming into the organization meets agreed data standards so that it is appropriately formatted and provides more informed analysis;

- *developing common data standards for the business*, in helping to define wider opportunities for the business;

- *Driving up quality and value through streamlined data quality and data acquisition services for the business*, by delivering one streamlined data acquisition service which manages the end to end process on behalf of the business; and

- *Ensuring data standards are managed, enforced, and continuously reviewed*, delivering consistency through data architectural tools such as enterprise analytics or cloud technology using the standards to help facilitate business level understanding and adherence.

There could be several reasons why companies wish to share data. The most likely examples are fraud prevention and compliance or legal purposes. For example, the car insurance sector routinely shares customer information to prevent fraudulent claims from the same person. To put this into context, the sudden rise in UK whiplash claims resulting from car accidents gave rise to numerous insurance investigations. In the end, the UK Government and car insurance industry decided it would be better to change legislation at one end and share customer data (even though they were likely to be in a competitor's market) rather than risk unduly paying out on fraudulent claims.[28]

In summary, we have seen several definitions of data and governance. Bringing the concepts together still creates some ambiguity. However, despite the varying approaches across strategic and operational practices, the critical factor underpinning any governance is clear communication across the business. Bringing changes through data governance actually presents a unique opportunity to bind business strategy and operational practice together. Weaving together both approaches provides the business with a more coherent process of strategic decision making.

---

[28] https://bit.ly/2f4Nhuy. (Accessed 21/06/2017).

To ensure data governance is successful, the business will need to deliver a clear communication strategy across the business – sending out the signal that improved governance will encourage growth of confident data which can benefit the business overall.

Data confidence

Achieving confident data means using tools (standards, strategy, and policies) to clearly align business objectives with realistic IT deliverables and produce meaningful outcomes. Having clear data governance embedded within the organization will create a better environment to cultivate and grow confident data. Confident data prioritizes accuracy and quality, ensuring that the organization can trust information being produced.

A key objective is to make the business recognize the asset value of data both in strategic and practical terms. How is this achieved? From a strategic perspective, we can sell the benefits of higher quality data to improve the results of analytics which lead to better informed management decisions. From practical terms, this covers mastering data management tools and bespoke storage solutions such as the cloud.

From a data perspective, financial yield increases are most likely going to be realized sometime after the technology investment. From a financial perspective, not being able to see immediate results can make Finance Directors nervous. This is where effectively selling benefits of data without a clear governance strategy becomes increasingly challenging.

So how do we get data to a position of confidence? There are several steps that are required:

- **Have a data strategy that charts the business direction over a period.** Strategy charts the direction for a business as it continues to evolve. This is often described in high level abstract terms and is usually the easiest to grasp. Data strategy sets out its alignment to business vision over the next few years. During this period, the business will usually commit to a process of change, some radical, some not. In any event, the main objective for a strategy is to set the course of direction across an unfamiliar landscape. Your strategy could be in the form of a short document explaining the benefits and charting the journey towards the organization's ultimate goals.

- **Explain the value of data to future business.** Data means different things to different people. In the purest business sense, data should be recognized as a vital commodity. To a business, having customer data that is accurate provides opportunities for targeted marketing via personalized social platform interaction, better quality data analytics to trial new innovations and most importantly getting to know your customers' behavior better. Understanding individual profiles also allows businesses the chance to establish sustained loyalty by delivering more of what the customer wants in the medium to long term. In other words, having better customer data means more chance of retaining customer loyalty.

- **Find a senior sponsor.** You'll need to find a senior sponsor committed to supporting this level of organizational transformation at a Board level. If you convince the Finance department and its Directors of the future longer-term benefits and leverage its support, you have a greater chance of success. Again, that's not to say that other senior sponsors won't be able to successfully push through the proposed changes; they certainly can. In some respects, the more senior buy-in acquired, the easier it will be to implement a data transformation.

- **Endorse data governance as the tool that binds high level strategy and operational process together.** Having a clear strategy is useful in setting out the direction for the future. But, if a strategy isn't supported by clear data governance or doesn't acknowledge the importance of operational tools (such as data quality or data mastery), it's merely only a high-level aspirational statement. In other words, strategic recognition of data will help increase organizational awareness and confidence of data as an asset. Specific hard coded solutions aren't required at this stage since business requirements may evolve as an organization travels down the road of change. What is essential, however, is having the flexibility to respond to changing circumstances as they arise. The scope of a data governance system should accommodate flexibility to allow for critical decision making at senior levels where necessary.

- **Build an effective data governance function.** There are a few factors that are needed to build a data governance function. This includes a fully engaged Executive Board committed to data governance. Firstly, the most important aspect is to ensure senior stakeholders are supportive with the strategic direction of the business. Promoting the benefits of effective data governance in the longer term is something that businesses and executives alike will find difficult to dismiss outright. An effective data governance function also includes getting the balance right between technical, strategic, and managerial expertise. Even though the subject matter is likely to be data-related, there will be a need for other expert views to be present. The size of the company will play a role in determining who will be present at the data governance board. If the company is small, all key decision-makers are likely to be present. If the organization has a well-established IT function, one might expect the data governance board to be composed of more technically-focused decision makers such as from Finance, Operations, IT and Data. Although a data governance board and an executive board may appear like duplication or management inefficiency, there is a distinction between the two forums. The data governance board is focused more on technical aspects of data-related issues. The main executive board will be focusing on broader management and strategic issues.

The creation and development of data governance and standards is one thing but ensuring compliance can be a different thing all together. Impartiality, integrity, and promoting innovation are qualities that are fundamental to any board.

One way of capturing board member consensus is to *create terms of reference and a mandate that each person subscribes to.* Here is an example of standard terms of reference for a meeting:

Terms of Reference Structure (Draft)
- Scope – clearly stating the remit of the Board and its functions.
- Purpose – what the Board is responsible for in terms of governance and assurance.
- Accountability – states whom or what governance this Board reports to or is held accountable.
- Membership – specifies how committee members will be appointed to the Board, listing the full membership of Board members and other attendees. This section will also provide details of reappointments or resignations.
- Administration – covers reporting and functioning of the Board and its committee.
- Frequency of Meetings – clearly states how often the Board should meet.
- Quorum – defines the rules for majority voting and chairing for audit purposes.
- Duties and responsibilities – stating what actions and decisions the Board is expected to take and on behalf of whom.
- Board Member Responsibilities – is used to illustrate the responsibilities and behaviors required.
- Monitoring effectiveness of Board – states how the Board will monitor its effectiveness by reviewing and reporting on its performance.
- Review – states the frequency for review of the Terms of Reference.

This Terms of Reference structure illustrates the type of power a data governance board is likely to exhibit across the organization. It has been developed using a standard or generic type format.[29] The most important point is to create a terms of reference document that meets the organization's data governance requirements.

Data ethics

Given the tendency for people to seek out simplicity, the behavior of the board and its members could be rolled up into the term "data ethics." Although captured in the above terms of reference, it is important to ensure that board members act ethically when handling sensitive data matters.

Data ethics is inextricably linked to data governance although there is a slight distinction between the two. Data governance focuses on effective tools and structures available to manage the use of data and meet strategic goals of the organization. Data ethics is linked to the emergence of new technologies that can produce, analyze, and interpret data automatically and at great speeds. Given most data capture is likely to be personal

---

[29] Here a simple Internet search for Committee meeting templates will provide a number of examples that can be used to model against your own organization.

identifiable information, it poses significant questions around the control and management of these automated systems.

The ethical impact of technology has crept up on data analytics and data science as a whole. How should one behave when using customer information, particularly when the sophisticated algorithm development is available and can be used for potential psychological profiling at unprecedented scale?

The risks associated with profiling social media data stores are being played out publicly through the likes of Cambridge Analytica and Facebook to name a few. Data sharing is not considered to be an illegal activity, provided there are enough safeguards in place for the capture and distribution of customer information. The use of secure technology is available; the question is whether sharing information itself becomes ethically acceptable.

The terms of reference example above make reference to data governance board members acting in an ethical way. But just what do we mean by ethics? The dictionary definition is based around morality and behaviors: *"Moral principles that govern a person's behavior or the conducting of an activity."* [30] In the context of data, the philosophical question is whether a person who has access to personal

---

[30] Dictionary definition of Ethics; Oxford English Dictionary; https://bit.ly/2N83m5p (accessed 23/02/2018).

identifiable information should disclose the information, even though its contents may have unintended effects.

There should be a symbiotic relationship between the organization and data governance. The objective is to provide the business with an effective data function. As the function matures, the aim is to establish a series of data standards that set the highest benchmarks. The theory is that creating ambitious standards will drive up quality and performance. Data standards can also be used collectively to help measure the progress of a company and its journey through data compliance and best practice.

In terms of delivery, we have seen how the creation of a data governance board helps the organization understand the scope and remit when using data. In terms of moving to a more tactical level of detail, using data quality standards and data mastering management tools will help the organization achieve a position of data confidence. Implementing a data governance system to bridge strategy and operations provide senior decision-makers with increased transparency across the business.

This chapter has outlined the importance of data governance and its benefits to the organization. Having found senior support and the backing of the Finance department to start the journey, let's get things moving! The next chapter, Getting Data Fit, begins to explore the basic elements needed to implement effective data governance.

CHAPTER 4

Getting Data Fit

This section will look at the basic elements required to make data governance work. Using a simple cookbook analogy, the recipe steps required include:

1. a clear aspiration or high-level goal;
2. principles derived from a clear strategy;
3. gaps identified by testing the strategy against current business practices;
4. operational plan for delivery; and
5. prototype different models and test thoroughly.

The idea is to follow these steps thoroughly, and let settle and bake well until all the data layers have formed properly in a uniform manner! Of course, the things shown on cookery TV channels don't necessarily look like things produced in real life! However, the main objective of this chapter is to build an understanding of the requirements and approaches used to establish a robust data governance system.

Let's apply these five steps to our case study. For this example, we will consider our fictitious mid-sized organization called D474 that embarks upon data governance.

The case of D474 and data governance using the 5-step method

D474's data is being held by business areas with no centralized control or repository function. The absence of a centralized function has caused each individual business area to develop and maintain its bespoke set of data controls.

From a data governance perspective, there is a wider risk of duplicate information being stored unnecessarily. It is costly and highly ineffective. With business areas capturing information to serve their own requirements, it becomes increasingly challenging to see beyond the siloed perimeters and nearly impossible to visualize a whole business view. When visibility of the entire business view becomes impaired, now is the time to reflect upon the steps set out in the data governance methodology as mentioned above.

Step 1) a clear aspiration or high-level goal

This is effectively defining the organizational ambition. In the case of D474, the myriad of data silos is a risk to the whole business. Your aspiration statement should resonate and meet business needs.

In terms of risk mitigation, the aspiration for D474 is to *create and implement a centralized system of data governance.* This will be the clear, high level aspiration for the organization. By articulating what the data ambition is, indirectly, the target goal for data governance is defined as well. Once the aspirational statement is defined, it must be agreed to by all key stakeholders. Engaging stakeholders to seek agreement will be a frequent process throughout, so it is essential to build good relationships. Naturally the types of communication will vary between stakeholders. It will be up to you to decide which medium is most appropriate. The more senior the stakeholder, the greater requirement for formalized communication. Essential tools to spread the message include emails, briefings, papers, polls, visuals, workshops, and meetings.

How do you get the aspirational statement out there? Quite simply, by using all the communication tools you have. As mentioned above, internal communications will have a variety of methods. The key is to ensure the message is heard loud and clear. The business will have a deeper understanding of daily operations and intuitively be able to spot flaws or gaps in any strategic design.

As the aspirational statement begins to take hold, the preferred communication style for each type of stakeholder will also start to emerge. It is important to document stakeholder preferences as this will be useful especially when seeking quick response turnarounds. So, you've managed to identify your key stakeholders using the appropriate communication tools to get the clear message out. As a result, you've got agreement on defining the end goal.

Congratulations on reaching the first step, which is normally (in most aspects of life) the most difficult to take! Now that you have a clear message underpinning the strategic direction as discussed earlier, this on its own is not enough. Having gained the confidence of senior management, it is important to sustain interest and keep them apprised of progress. This brings us quite neatly to the next step.

Step 2) developing principles from a clear strategy

This step is crucial. Having an end goal established provides you with the essential tool to carve out a clear strategy. But what does a clear strategy looks like? The impetus of an end goal message also provides you with a clearer scope to define what that strategy may contain.

The clear message is effectively a strapline that is a concise statement about the data strategy. Data strategy is important because it sets out the future direction for the organization. Data strategy could be framed in terms of a map plotting out delivery time or a short paper.

Let's say a business objective for D474 is to *"Create and implement a centralized system of data governance."* Using this clear statement of intent, we can start to develop some more detail around this message. For example, *"the objective for D474 is to establish the vision for a centralized governance function to lead and direct the delivery of data-related matter across the organization. In this context, the delivery of data-related matters means definition, development, and implementation of data services, data strategy, and data management."* It is important to be clear about scope and definition to ensure everyone understands the messaging!

Establishing the strategic ambition

Understanding the strategic ambition can be challenging, particularly if the responsibility for deciphering it is derived from a carefully worded statement. Playback your understanding to other to ensure you and your intended audience are talking about the same thing.

Using common terms that are known across industry is one way of handling a potentially tricky issue. It will usually turn out to be a combination of best practices filtered into a bespoke process that is tailored specifically to the company.

Does the strategy focus on a little or a lot? Is the strategic ambition of the organization aimed correctly? These can be a challenge to get right. Often, the strategic ambition of any company is a statement about delivering high value for customers and shareholders. Potentially there may also be a reference to harnessing technology to achieve this goal. To capture all elements, strategic statements can be set quite granular. Although this can be helpful in some context when mapping against a data governance framework, the flip side of a low-level strategy is that it becomes too narrowly entrenched in one area and therefore less sighted in other key strategic areas.

What about scope? Organizations are generally driven by growing company value in terms of customers, shareholders, goodwill, and revenue. The other key areas include managing regulatory compliance in an effective manner and delivering cost efficiency and savings wherever possible. Given these are general tenets that most organizations will recognize, the question is where does data governance fit in?

In simple terms, the answer is *all of the above*. Data governance is the process that provides the controls and assurance the business needs to meet the operational functions and demands of a data-driven organization. The scope of data governance is likely to support one if not all the general tenets mentioned. The next step is to formulate a strategy from the high-level end goal. Once this is done we can then start to build data principles.

Developing principles is how the business begins to understand the scale and impact of change. Data governance principles are statements of intent that commit the organization to future behavior. Drawing from the aspiration statement we start to design a strategy. The strategy then in turn supports the development of core data principles.

What are data principles?

For the purposes of our case study, the data principles should be clear, concise, and scoped wide enough to cover all data activity. Taking a simple housebuilding analogy, imagine that data principles are similar to core foundations becoming pillars that will support and deliver stable governance. Data principles are statements of intent that commit the business to better data governance activity. Data governance for D474 will:

- Capture, store, retain, and manage data for the benefit of the organization (setting scope);

- Use technology and tools to maintain the highest standards of quality (use of data analytics, cleansing and profiling) to deliver accurate and confident data;

- Create a policy-making function which will oversee legal, handling and security requirements over data use, extraction; and

- Produce relevant guidance and raise business awareness related to data responsibilities and accountabilities.

At first glance these statements appear pitched at a remarkably high level. However, this is the intent! The reality is that data principles are likely to be scoped with the widest definitions in mind. But how did we get to this point and what was the approach taken to create the above principles? The next section explores the approach in further detail.

When drafting or scoping principles, it is important to think about a few issues to help with drafting guidelines for principles:

- What is the principle? It is important to think about a specific issue or title.

- Why is this principle a potential problem? You should be thinking about summarizing the concern, concept, or issue.

- How will you address the issue? The principle should be able to summarize the process or activity undertaken to resolve or mitigate.

- What is the intended outcome? You should be able to describe the result and benefit of these actions.

It's important to remember that the principles should be pitched at the appropriate level. Anything too detailed will be difficult for the audience to digest quickly, and anything too high level will not catch the attention of decision makers.

Data principles are not just important for underpinning the strategy above – they also support the detailed framework below. The further we travel downwards towards operations, the more detail about the process is required.

There is no doubt that a new ecosystem focused on data is evolving at a quick pace. As new technologies continue to provide new opportunities to harness the power of data, the need for a stable structure or framework is essential.

Step 3) testing the strategy against current business practices to identify gaps

Testing is a word that is frequently used for many different things. In the IT world it is usually linked to software development. However, in this context, testing simply means checking the robustness of your strategy. Test to see if it works. If exposed to a live environment, is the strategy stable enough to meet business demands under pressure?

Within Agile and SDLC software development life cycles, testing is a fundamental process that checks the validity of the product. Within a data governance context, we want to ensure that the strategic model encompasses all data-related matters and brings this together in a coordinated manner.

Does the strategy meet its intended objective? Here, we know the aim is to move away from disparate methods and bring a standardized approach to data management. We also know that moving from a multi-faceted and complex environment into a new world of a standardized set of rules and controls designed to bring order, isn't going to happen overnight.

Being realistic about the scope and time of impact is just as important as saying you can deliver a particular milestone. It might not be what everyone wants to hear but being honest throughout the process is just as important. It allows you to manage stakeholder expectations more effectively and fosters a more open and constructive relationship.

Are all our stakeholders on board? Although this may appear to be a simple yes or no answer, it isn't in practice.

Updating key stakeholders is normally the domain of project managers, architects, and business leads. It may require all three elements depending on the size of the company. In the case of D474, we know the key principles have already been discussed with stakeholders and have been approved. Ensuring the next step requires the same level of approval and while firing off an email may save time, it may not have the same impact as bringing stakeholders together for a conference call or meeting.

So, we've identified the gaps in this step. What now?

Step 3 focuses on testing the strategy to ensure it is robust enough to sustain a live environment. Being an optimist, I would like to think that *your strategy is sound enough* given all the requirement gathering and analysis done in the initial phase of development.

However, what happens if this isn't the case and there are still gaps in the process? It is worth returning to the previous step to review. For example, there may be a gap between user stories or customer journeys and IT needs to gather hard business requirements at a more granular level. Drawing together high-level user stories and business requirements is no easy task. Often it requires revisiting and challenging assumptions to ensure there is agreement reached across all sides on approach and definitions. This may feel monotonous and repetitive. However, the reinvested time spent on gap analysis will help to ensure that data governance implementation is focused on the appropriate areas at the right time.

If we take the case of D474 for example, we know that this is the first time the company is embarking on a data governance implementation and therefore we should expect some gaps to occur.

As the data governance model matures within the organization, we expect the gaps to reduce naturally over time. The reason for this natural gap reduction is because over time, the governance model will be more emended within the organization. D474's people will be more familiar with the new approach and be able to add more input. Furthermore, it would allow the business to refine the data governance model in a way that is better suited to its strategic priorities at the time.

Step 4) build out an operational plan for delivery

The definition of "build out" in this context is to develop with a wide focus. One could put forward an argument that the best laid plans are those that are narrow in scope, clear and well executed. Most plans that tick all the above are usually founded on a simple aim. For example, deliver an update to all key stakeholders by the end of the month.

This is not to say that the work that goes into drafting, circulating, and presenting an update becomes an oversight. These tasks become integral to the plan itself.

Keeping track of progress as things become more complex inevitably becomes more complex. There are many well tested methods and approaches that are available to manage the process of planning. Given each company is different, the plan for delivery is also likely to differ (and rightly so!). Each company has its own identity and will have differing requirements.

For the purpose of illustration, we will use D474 to explain what is meant by building out an operational plan in this instance. Firstly, it is important not to confuse what is considered strategic and what is considered operational. With regards to D474, the strategic plan is the overarching ambition that charts a direction for the organization's future. Here we know that D474's objective is to develop a well-defined data governance model that can support the company.

The operational plan takes the high-level principles established from the strategic plan and starts to consider how these can be achieved in practice. In terms of delivery, the operational goals will be set at a lower level. If D474 has several different functions including Finance, Operations, Digital, IT, Policy, Legal, Compliance, HR, and Marketing, operationally the planning will need to include all these diverse functions working collaboratively to meet the goal of embedded data governance. This may involve breaking down the strategic plan and evaluating each principle.

Who takes responsibility for developing these operational plans? Given that the focus is at department/group level, each function could take responsibility for delivering its own operational plan. Depending on the size of your organization, the head of the IT/Finance department would take overall responsibility for reporting and delivery of an operational plan. In the case of D474, each business head will ensure an operational plan is produced.

Quite simply, this could be done by asking the following question: What do these changes mean for each area of the business? Finance and Legal teams may be impacted differently by the strategic changes proposed. How will a fully-fledged data governance model affect the daily workings of these departments? These perspectives of lower level impacts will be captured by the operational plans.

Once these impacts have been captured by the business areas, it is important to take a step back and reflect. The impacts may be a combination of positive and negative comments but the key point here is to understand the triggers behind these statements. The triggers are the things that cause someone to react in a particular way. Of course, there are potentially a million reasons why people respond to the same thing in different ways. The most common triggers tend to be environmental, social, or behavioral.

Impact assessments provide a helpful tool into the current state of the organization. When looking to implement your data governance system, the most important thing is to communicate and plan effectively! Developing an operational plan that effectively charts the end to end implementation lifecycle, will help to ensure that key stakeholders and interested parties are kept informed of progress.

Step 5) prototype different models and test thoroughly

The last step in this process is arguably the most challenging one to get right. The business is armed with all the relevant information needed to make a decision and move forward. The risk analysis and costings would have been produced for each of the following data governance options. The billion-dollar question is "What is the best data governance option to deploy: prototype, build, or buy?"

As with typical software implementation approaches, a similar process is likely to follow the implementation of a data governance system. By prototyping different models, the organization can then make an informed decision as to what works best.

The option to build can be useful depending on the organization's size and its technology capability. Larger organizations may have in house IT capability and introducing bespoke automated data systems are likely to be more suitable. In this scenario, commercial off-the-shelf packages will not be designed to meet the requirements for a large and often complex organization. It might be that a simple commercial off-the-shelf product could meet all requirements. If it doesn't, enhancements are required.

The final decision is for the executive board to make. The architect may wish to make recommendations or influence the debate but that's as far it is likely to go. The financial considerations and value for money debate could indeed be discussed at a Data Governance Board level. However, it is more appropriate for the Data Governance Board to pass its findings and recommendations on to the Executive Board as final decision maker.

In the case of D474, the organization has several sections all performing similar data management functions. We know there is likely inefficiencies with the current approach, because of the risk of sections duplicating actions.

With any organizational review, our approach is to eliminate duplicate practices and ensure that one area, section, or team takes sole responsibility for a specific role or group of actions. This frees up valuable time for other areas and allows management to refocus, retrain, and allocate resources to other parts of the organization.

Establishing a data framework for governance

Using the data principles to group and reorganize data management tasks is an opportunity to test as many permutations with key stakeholders as possible before reaching an agreement. You may find that some parts of the organization will not take kindly to the proposed changes. Those groups who might be performing similar roles will more likely resist giving up expertise functions to a central part of the organization. Clear stakeholder management will be required to work through potentially challenging conversations.

In my experience, I've found delivering news of change is never easy. Some people embrace change, others are more reluctant. Communicating openly and honestly about the process is fundamental. By process, I mean explaining what changes are likely to happen as transformation begins to take effect. Trying to set out potential changes that might never occur can be unnecessarily risky. I once heard the term "unknown unknowns" and was often baffled about its usage, but I think the term might fit in this scenario. It can be a challenge talking in abstract terms when your audience is looking for factual content!

I've also found that being open (or brutally honest at times) about *why* the organization must change is important. Setting out the context and laying management options on the table, helps the larger workforce better understand the need for change. If the context for transformation is not provided, there is likely to be greater resistance in the long run. When faced with different questions, I've been honest enough to say "I don't know" but endeavor to find out at a later stage and communicate back.

Given that any data transformation activity is likely to submit a realistic view of the organization, uncomfortable or not, it is worth making everyone aware of the journey. The road ahead may not be smooth but it's important to make everyone aware of its potential pitfalls as well as its benefits.

Effective implementation of data governance requires a collective effort by the business to recognize the asset value of data and make changes needed to realize a centralized information process that benefits the entire organization. As mentioned earlier, there are many data governance models and definitions available.

Having the best interests of the organization in mind is the common denominator that brings staff and affiliates together. Ensuring the business can flourish in the current climate of economic uncertainty is something that is critical for the company to survive. Planning future strategy to ensure not only survival but continued success is a fundamental driver for all parts of the business. To remain competitive and robust as a business, any opportunity to maximize or leverage an edge or asset is critical. In the same way, drawing upon all the data available within the organization can help support future business strategy.

The challenge for most organizations is that moving rapidly towards a desired outcome is risky without a clear plan or strategy. In other words, the preferred approach by many organizations is to adopt a step-by-step approach towards change. Why is this approach more suitable than a complete overhaul? To ensure all stakeholders are on board. You may not know the exact destination but if you are able to point out the direction that is better than nothing. As most organizations take tentative first steps into the unknown, a practical and pragmatic approach will help deal with those challenges that may arise.

In addition, and equally as important, adopting a practical approach provides the flexibility to either immediately deal with or postpone any issues that come to light. The decision to resolve or postpone issues for a later date is a matter for the governance structure in place at the time of discovery. For example, if D474 discovered that it did not have the skills or capabilities in terms of workforce available to deliver effective data governance, the existing management structure, in this case the executive board, could defer data governance implementation until it has acquired the necessary personnel required to deliver this change.

In contrast, attempting a complete overhaul is a bit like introducing sudden disruption to an existing system to bring about a change in behavioral pattern or process. The objective is to see immediate results or benefits when presented with a new challenge. The exception is that people will adapt more quickly to managing a sudden change in environment or process. Although in theory this short, sharp, shock treatment may prove tempting to some, changing business practices and people's attitudes towards change can be met with uncertainty, resistance, or worse still rejection!

What is a framework?

We are hearing the term "framework" more frequently within the IT industry. As with most buzzwords, this term appears to have had a renaissance! In simple terms a framework is the structure that holds things together.

The Oxford English Dictionary has a more refined explanation, *"An essential supporting structure of a building, vehicle, or object. A basic structure underlying a system, concept, or text."*[31]

To provide context to this definition, I like the car chassis analogy; it provides the underpinning structure for the axles which connect to the wheels. It's the chassis that provides support to other components such as the engine and body. Similarly, the framework for data provides the structure to support the entire governance model. The framework is an attempt to move from strategic thinking, which might be considered abstract at times, in to a physical world where goals begin to materialize. In the real world, this simple and clear message can often get lost in technical speak. I've often heard terms like "tangible deliverables", "workable outputs", and "concrete milestones." The wonderful lexicon of terms within Project Management, Consulting, and IT industries can be baffling at the best of times!

Putting a data framework under the microscope periodically is valuable because it allows focus on specific areas. Under closer inspection, a data framework should provide further clarity on the roles and functions that operate within its broader governance model. Arguably the most important reference material for a data governance framework stems from the seminal work by

---

[31] Oxford English Dictionary definition of Framework; https://bit.ly/2G2dGZA (accessed 23 October 2017).

the Data Governance Institute. The framework is essential reading and provides an excellent overview of data governance requirements. The Data Governance Institute defines the term framework as *"a logical structure for classifying, organizing, and communicating complex activities involved in making decisions about and taking action on enterprise data."*[32] Managing data at the enterprise level can only be sustained by a governance platform of standardized controls and processes.

---

[32] Data Governance Framework; DGI; https://bit.ly/2bQ5Ynh accessed 20/06/17.

CHAPTER 5

Data Governance Stakeholders

Whenever there is a need to introduce something new to existing processes, you can always assume that some resistance is lurking around the corner. Introducing something potentially disruptive like a data governance program could result in the organization rejecting the function outright. How can one address this concern? First seek executive agreement for the data governance function. Usually the selling points for a data governance function involve persuading management of the following:

- **Efficiency**. Streamlining data operations by creating uniformed processes means that a) duplicated events and governance can be eliminated, and b) the removal of silos within an organization means that local practices will also cease which will reduce spikes of variations and bring down potential costs to rectify. Developing a uniformed (one efficient way that is universally approved) process reduces waste and helps companies become fitter and more flexible in approach.

- **Company value or goodwill.** Persuading finance directors that implementing a data governance function will bring a higher return of investment. Why is this a challenge? The simple reason is that finance directors are overly cautious about anything IT related. Data purists might become infuriated at reading the next few sentences but unfortunately the fact is data and IT projects are often thought of as one and the same. Most Finance Directors and their departments are likely to have epic stories of an IT project that was heavily funded but still had the ignominy of spectacular failure. The thought of investing in an IT project that could end up hemorrhaging costs, is likely to have even the most supportive of Finance Officers on the defensive. To overcome this challenge, demonstrate a return of investment by reducing costs and introducing a uniformed approach to managing data across the business. Introducing a data governance function would help to identify potential gaps. This type of risk mitigation would be preventative in nature but also help stop any remedial costs at source before they potentially escalate out of control. The key to winning support in the finance world is to demonstrate that reducing duplication and removing complex processes (simplifying business rules) will help to make the company more efficient in its output. More efficient production will help increase savings and reduce expenditure which in this economic climate will sound inviting to the most frugal of finance departments.

The data governance function should be self-contained in its capacity to resolve issues swiftly but there is a recognition that it would need to report into the wider executive board. There are two ways it could potentially do this; 1) report upwards through an executive board member, such as via the corporate finance or IT work stream, or 2) have the data governance director sit on the executive board and report directly. Option 2) might be the more attractive choice because having a director for data governance sit on an executive board would provide wider recognition and acknowledgment of the importance of data. This director could also help put an end to the misunderstanding that data and IT are one and the same thing!

The basis for a data governance system will require some if not all the following elements set out in the diagram on the following page.

Data Privacy and Security is placed in the center of the diagram because it is the common element that crosses all other elements. Data privacy and security is a key component of data governance and therefore should be considered in each element. The following provides a short summary of each data governance element.

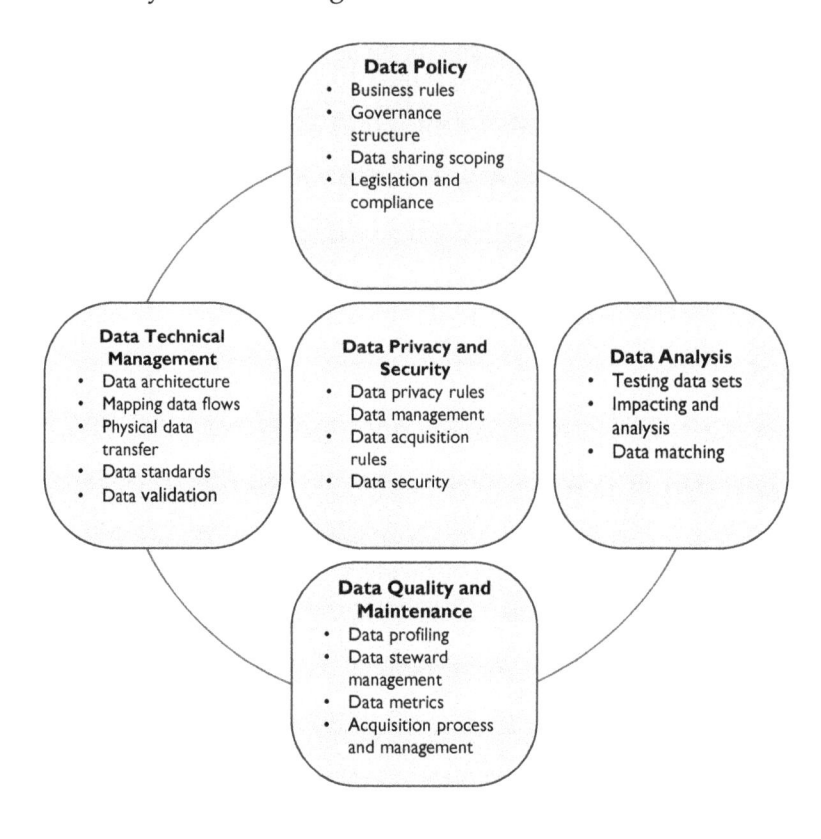

Data Policy
- Business rules
- Governance structure
- Data sharing scoping
- Legislation and compliance

Data Technical Management
- Data architecture
- Mapping data flows
- Physical data transfer
- Data standards
- Data validation

Data Privacy and Security
- Data privacy rules
- Data management
- Data acquisition rules
- Data security

Data Analysis
- Testing data sets
- Impacting and analysis
- Data matching

Data Quality and Maintenance
- Data profiling
- Data steward management
- Data metrics
- Acquisition process and management

Data policy

When writing a policy paper, one *must* get the structure and content flowing in a logical way. The easiest way to do this is to use a standardized outline:

- **Introduction**. Summarize the subject and issue, and know your audience as this can change the level of technical language in the paper.

- **Problem statement or proposal**. Define the problem and proposal in one sentence. Imagine the elevator pitch and having to state what the issue is quickly and succinctly.

- **Approach**. Tell the reader what action you intend to take. Demonstrate what will be needed for remedial action and how you will be anticipating any potential pitfall areas. One might want to set out a range of options and highlight the pros and cons for each of those options.

- **Expected outcomes**. Offer statistics, factors, and figures to emphasize your point to the audience.

- **Conclusion**. Briefly summarize the issue and provide recommendations. The conclusion is also the section where one can ask the audience to make a decision.

Data analysis

Data analysis provides the tools for users to understand complex data sets or management information (MI).

Technology has advanced the capability to securely store vast amounts of data using the cloud for example. However, data analysis provides users with greater functionality to transform, manage and direct information more effectively.

There are several data analysis functions:

- **Testing data sets**. This analysis applies to both structured and unstructured data. Structured usually means a logical flow of information and captured in a pre-defined block or record by the organization. All data capture in this approach follows the designated fixed format. Unstructured data in this regard refers to files which do not follow a standardized format but could form a combination of different data or media types (MP4 or JPEG for example).

- **Impacting and analysis**. This area is the mainstay of data science. Essentially this is the practice of analyzing data using a variety of tools, techniques, and applications to draw new (or previously unknown) information within existing datasets that can help organizations make more informed decisions.

- **Data matching**. Another technique used to manage large segments of information. Running queries for matches across different data stores can often be used to mine for information. The collective gathering of matched data can help to build a user or customer profile. This data mining practice is likely to be impacted by greater transparency and legislative requirements on the way customer data is profiled. Data matching helps to reduce duplication and redundancy across the organization.

Data quality and maintenance

Under this element, there are several functions that are used to manage and monitor data quality across the organization:

- **Data profiling.** The profiling of data is about the collection of statistical and technical characteristics about a particular data source. Effectively it is about measuring the quality of metadata and how that matches up to existing data standards. Any gaps or derivation in the data would then be analyzed further to understand the anomalies against the organization's data standards.

- **Data steward management.** The management and monitoring of data steward activity across the organization. Data stewards effectively mirror data governance activity in several ways: 1) establishing effective relationships with the business to build data governance understanding at an enterprise level, 2) working across the business to ensure there are clear guidelines and documentation in the use and management of the organization's data storage and system functions, and 3) ensuring compliance with organizational data standards.

- **Data metrics**. This is linked to the performance and output of data. In other words, the time taken to access information from the data stores and monitor statistical information on query and execute functionality.

- **Acquisition process and management**. While the data acquisition rules may be aligned to the data privacy element below, this relates to the actual process and management of third party acquisitions. Often data acquisitions also require commercial/financial oversight as some form of payment is made between parties. Acquisition process includes the business position on third party data use. This may require a degree of system flexibility (either policy or IT infrastructure related) as existing processes may need adjustments to accept new information. Other examples may include sharing of the organization's data standards criteria, the amount of data that is to be exchanged, and ensuring the technical requirements are clearly documented in the legally binding contract between parties.

Data technical management

The term technical management describes a number of functional areas. Each function has its own set of requirements. These are described below:

- **Data architecture**. This is about rules, policies and procedures involved in the capture and design of data models. These data models will be capturing different levels of interaction across the organization. The enterprise or conceptual data model will look at processes at the highest level.

- **Architectural models or views**. This help the business understand current processes at different layers or views. For example, a logical model goes several layers deeper to look at the logical transactions between systems and how messages are transmitted. Architectural models exist at all levels of the organization (business, logical, solution and infrastructure).

- **Data standards**. Architects will also be involved in the creation and maintenance of data standards. Data standards are essentially quality benchmarks designed to bring a uniformed and consistent approach to the use of data across the organization.

- **Mapping data flows.** This work stream considers if existing processes can be further improved, and analyzing physical data transfers to see if gaps in data standards occur.

- **Physical data transfer.** This area is about the physical components (or hardware) used to transmit information.

- **Data validation.** Architects will also be involved in data validation, which involves checking information systems to ensure data integrity remains consistent throughout the end to end process.

Data privacy and security

For the purposes of this book, data privacy and data security are brought together in this functional area. It might be easier to consider data privacy as a business management process that ensures controls over personal identifiable information (PII). Data security is about using technology safeguards to ensure information is always protected but accessible under the right credentials and permissions. Business management of data privacy will also be dependent upon robust data security technology being available. There are several Data privacy and security functions:

- **Data privacy rules and management.** The management of data privacy is about the use of PII which may be stored by a website, business, government body, or a third party. The type of personal information that could fall under data privacy rules are generally medical or financial related data. There is a case to say this could be wrapped up into the data policy element given the close alignment between the two areas. However, separating these out is helpful as it allows the wider organization to understand the importance of the subject matter. The use of data and maintaining data privacy is enshrined in legislation. Government, organizations, and third parties are obliged to comply with the rules governing data privacy and the disclosure of personalized identifiable information. The degree of legislation varies from country to country. Some countries may rely on industry self-regulation; other jurisdictions may require greater transparency and controls.

- **Data acquisition rules.** This includes when an organization buys or receives data from a third party. The actual process of data acquisition is covered under data quality and management. Here, the rules of data acquisition are likely to be aligned to data privacy rules in the handling and processing of information. The care and attention given to internal data is also required for using third party information.

- **Data security**. Keeping data protected using digital technology is a core function for all companies irrespective of size or stature. There are many ways that technology is used to protect data. One of the most common approaches to data security is the use of authentication to ensure data is kept secure. For example, to access information from a particular source, (say a data store in this case) a password or verification/validation step is required.

We will now turn to another useful tool to establish data governance effectiveness – the Data Governance Scorecard.

Data Governance Scorecard

A scorecard captures the effectiveness of a particular approach or application. For this section, we will focus on the function of data governance. Here, each question is marked according to its maturity level within the organization. The maturity levels range from none to high with a score of 0-10. A mark of 10 is the highest score.

A Data Governance Scorecard can be used at any point in time to check for data governance effectiveness. The benefit of using a scorecard is that it provides a clear and transparent view of the different areas of data governance. The maturity level score can also help senior management understand, at a glance, where the strengths and weaknesses are in terms of data governance development. Quality, policy, and security functions can be aligned and provide greater understanding of how things should be integrated. The scorecard is a valuable tool for reporting requirements to management.

As with most things, there should be care exercised when using a scorecard. It is important to remember this should be used to encourage performance and not be used to target low levels directly. Teams and business areas may mark differently; some may opt for higher scores, whereas others may be harder and give lower markings. It is important that these variances are used as a general guide and help to kick-start more detailed and structured conversations.

The scorecard provides a useful framework for strategic conversations, it helps identify pressure points and map the maturity levels of a data governance system at any time.

Data Governance Scorecard					
		\multicolumn{4}{c}{**Maturity Level**}			
\multicolumn{2}{l}{**Data Governance Function Questions**}	None 0-2	Low 3-4	Med 5-7	High 8-10
1	Do you have a DG function in place?				
2	Does the DG function align with the strategic ambition of the organization?				
3	Does the DG function provide strategic direction, using tools such as a framework or blueprint for example?				
4	Is there a clear DG function that manages the daily operations of data within the business?				
5	Is there a DG Governance Board and terms of reference?				
6	Does the DG Governance Board comprise of members from all business areas?				
7	Is there clear accountability for data items at any given point within the organization?				
8	Is there a Data Privacy and Security function? For example, the management of data privacy rules, the management of dataflow/data assets within the organization, acquisition rules, and data security?				
9	Is there a Data Policy function? For example, setting business rules, managing DG Board matters, compliance, and scope for data sharing?				

Data Governance Scorecard					
		Maturity Level			
Data Governance Function Questions		None 0-2	Low 3-4	Med 5-7	High 8-10
10	Is there a Data Architecture function? For example, managing and handling data flows, data journeys, data models, data standards and validation.				
11	Is there a Data Quality function? For example, managing data acquisition, data metrics, data profiling and data acquisition.				
12	Is there a Data Analysis function? For example, testing data sets, providing impacting and analysis and data matching.				
13	Is there clear communication and understanding across the organization of data governance and data assets?				
14	Does everyone in the organization understand the important of data legislation and the personal responsibilities in case of a breach?				
	Totals				
	Grand Total				

We have looked at the components of a data governance framework. However, while these are all key elements that go into building effective machinery, it is equally important to look at things holistically. In other words, stepping back and looking at the system as a whole. Developing a bigger picture of governance and its purpose and place in the wider context will foster further understanding.

From here, we now turn towards more general approaches, practices, and methodologies that might be impacted by a data governance function.

Approaches, practices, and methodologies

An organization might consider both Agile and Waterfall approaches when looking to implement an IT or data governance function. We then look at the language of IT terminology and its evolution. The constant change in IT terminology means that it can be challenging trying to communicate your message, clearly and effectively across the organization.

Agile vs. Waterfall

Indeed, both Agile and Waterfall approaches have been successfully used across government and the private sector. As a result, both Agile and Waterfall have influenced and informed other spheres of industry. For example, project management methodologies such as

PRINCE (which was created by a UK government department)³³ has evolved into its own school of thought and have been successfully used by all sectors to implement programs and projects of all sizes.

Waterfall as a process, while sound in methodology, has received criticism for being too lengthy in terms of actual delivery time. The inability to go back a step made the process seem inflexible as it committed the organization to one solution at an incredibly early stage of design. This type of commitment could be regarded as challenging for organizations with stable systems that have evolved at a slower pace in comparison with other technologies.

An excellent summary of the Agile methodology and its application is provided by the Association for Project Management (APM) in the North West (of the UK). The APM's report focuses on the practical application of Agile, providing a neat history of the boom and bust years of information system application using both Agile and Waterfall.³⁴

Naturally the APM does favor the Agile methodology as the more sophisticated approach to adopt. The fail faster approach through sprints is now commonplace across

---

[33] Best Management Practice Portfolio: Guidance; Cabinet Office; Gov.UK; https://bit.ly/1SuoKYU (Accessed 21/10/17).
[34] The Practical Adoption of Agile Methodologies; The Association for Project Management, APM North West, 2015).

industry. Fail fast, fail often, has its benefits when considering initial scoping or looking at a bespoke project, which has defined delivery timelines. It means ideas can be explored more thoroughly within a short, fixed period. This provides users with the opportunity to drive forward ideas within a safe environment.

As mentioned earlier, the debate between Agile supporters and protagonists continues to rage. Some have questioned the key objectives behind Agile. Arguably the staunchest critique of Agile is found in Dronzek and Lanowitz's report entitled *The Agile Dilemma*.[35] This report caused quite a stir within the Agile camp suggesting it was a movement against unwanted tasks and schedules underpinned by a ploy to promote the Agile methodology or costly services.

Another quick Internet search will allow you to find a plethora of articles, journals, and reviews on why Agile works. Most agree on the following two key points:

- Rigid organizational structures cause teams to be less effective when using an Agile approach; and
- the typically seismic gap in understanding between DevOps (developers and operations) means that ideas carried forward are not practicable.

---

[35] The Agile Dilemma; Dronzek and Lanowitz; Voke, 2012. https://bit.ly/2QmPdDcAccessed 19/09/17.

Interestingly, there appears to be general agreement across both Agile and non-Agile camps that the smaller the project, the greater chances of success for Agile.

Another contentious area for Agile is the quantity of documentation produced when running through each sprint. Critics point out that producing documentation is not explicit and therefore lessons learned are not captured in a format that could be of some repository value. Repository value means having documentation that could be stored for future use.

Supporters of Agile would counter by pointing out that although the quantity of documentation may not be explicitly stated, it does not mean forget to document altogether! Rather, it means being selective and efficient about what is documented at each stage. Having captured the lessons of failing faster, it would serve as a reference for others considering similar ideas in the future.

The continual changing of requirements does not help the data architect who is tasked with trying to develop business requirements into IT solutions that are deliverable. What is the mitigation here? Clearly, the need is to agree to a firm set of requirements with stakeholders. This is where the diplomacy skills of the architect come into play. Eliciting key information is a skill that requires practice and development over time. There is a simple approach that is used but it is difficult to master. The approach is to challenge everything. Never take anything at face value, always seek documentary evidence to confirm or counter everything that has been said verbally.

The second part of the approach involves the word "why." Asking why helps you to cut through superfluous information and focus on the key elements. Rather like children, their inquisitive nature makes then ideal architects. Imagine if you will, a situation where a parent is trying to simplify a complex issue to a child. As the parent explains as clearly as possible, the child continues to ask why. Each time the parent is forced to consider a new response, (which after several repetitive cycles) is eventually refined until it cannot be broken down any further. Reaching this point is the nirvana for architects as it ensures no further distillation can occur, therefore the application/concept/issue/component can be captured accurately without further risk of amendment.

Often, the largest businesses are not agile enough to manage intensive change within a short space of time due to business complexity as opposed to driving faster organizational change. In other words, business rules require careful assessment before undertaking any change. This aspect is part of basic project management, but it is worth noting here. A data governance function would also consider any strategic implications or wider contingency risks to the business.

Agile is a practice that has become embedded within IT. In terms of data governance, it is important to recognize the benefits of different delivery mechanisms, particularly when testing and deploying new data-driven technology solutions. In summary, there are benefits for both Agile and Waterfall approaches. When looking to implement a data governance function, both methodologies can be equally important. The point here is that data governance is a fluid system and has the capacity to encompass any changes in approach, practice, or method.

Conducting thought showers in a bunker

While acknowledging the fluidity of data governance, there is another key component that continues to evolve – the use of IT terminology. This section picks up a few buzzwords to illustrate the point that whilst language might be new, the concepts behind the terms generally remain the same.

As technology evolves so does the art of its language. In the quest to deliver something novel, creative language is often used to convey the appeal of a new product or exciting concept. For example, we have looked at the Agile methodology which has now become the preferred method when conducting initial scoping sessions. These sessions were commonly known as "brainstorming" and now have evolved through political correctness to become known as "thought showers." Although language may have evolved to describe some of the concepts, I find that some of the processes are quite similar, if not the virtually same! I like to describe this as the evolution of the workshop.

The principle behind a workshop is to gather decision makers into one place and through discussion find a resolution. Often these discussions can get heated as people begin to debate issues. The intended outcome, of course, is to find common ground and reach agreement. Meetings remain the bedrock of facilitating important discussion. Variations on this theme have begun to appear in the IT space. Rather ironically, the term "bunker" which has its origins in historic military warfare, is now being used to describe intense discussion to reach agreement. In other words, lock the doors and throw away the keys until a resolution from all sides is found!

One could argue that presentations have been superseded by the concept of "market stalls." Just like a market selling goods and wares, these stalls allow people to wonder around and explore what's on offer. The "traders" are effectively skilled in the art of practical demonstrations articulating the latest trend or concept. The informal style of a market stall means you can have a relaxed conversation without the need for a formal boardroom setting.

Face to face interactions are still needed to provide a human touch and to ensure your audience understands the message. When data governance takes many forms and variations, it is important to convey a clear message and seek consensus with your audience.

Seeking consensus is the goal irrespective of the process used to get there. From a purist perspective, this approach could be regarded as too general. Purists are likely to take issue with the argument that workshops, brainstorming shower sessions, and bunkers could be considered one and the same thing.

Getting your core assumptions in order

It is imperative that your audience understand the message you wish to convey. Irrespective of the latest terminology or method used, if your audience has a different understanding from your own set of assumptions, it is unlikely that your goals will progress.

One challenge is making sure your audience understands what your intentions and objectives are at the onset. I'm assuming many of you will be able to recall a recent situation where some of your stakeholders have not been fully aware of the full proximity or scope of the situation. This can be a challenge, particularly if these stakeholders are senior decision-makers. A colorful array of idioms apply to these scenarios, but the simplest might be "getting all your ducks in a row." The main point here is that it is critical to ensure a universal and precise understanding of the issue from the very start.

Once the linguistic challenges have been overcome, it's time to ensure the core assumptions have been captured accurately. This requires the delicate art of balance in the following:

1. **Keeping an open mind**. The human condition leads people to judge situations based on previous experience. Although there may be parallels that can be drawn, each situation has its own unique set of characteristics. It is this unique set of factors which requires the most attention as this becomes the foundation for developing a strategy. It could be the business may want to enhance these characteristics to gain a competitive advantage. Or it might be the business wishes to transform from outdated practices to a technology which brings alive the power of data.

2. **Gathering requirements amid information overload (or not)**. It's challenging to pin down what the business actually requires, not what it *thinks* it needs. The business view can be considered insular, especially if the organization considers you to be the outsider looking in. When presented with a mass of information, more often it's about distilling relevant information from the superfluous. However, it can be equally difficult when dealing with no information at

all. Here the challenge is to agree to a set of requirements which may not have emanated from the business itself.

In short, it begins with validating your own core assumptions about the business with key stakeholders. Instincts and experience may lead to a certain viewpoint. However, this may not be in alignment with the business. To avoid any divergence from the start, be clear in your observations and assumptions.

If you don't understand the current buzzword or are lost in translation, don't be afraid to say so. It will save hours of trying to decipher something that may have just been an informal remark irrelevant to the task at hand. In summary, a need to have clear understanding across all data-related matters is the main driver for deciphering technical speak or breaking down complex information.

Data governance business drivers

In terms of business impacts, we have seen there are several social and economic factors driving the need for greater data management and monitoring of data-related functions. Social media platforms such as Facebook, Snapchat, and Instagram have pushed the boundaries of instant communication. Underpinning the vast technology stacks required to support social media platforms is the capture of data, including personal data.

Another key business driver is the uplift in mobile devices across the world. The number of global handheld devices surpassed the five billion mark in 2017 and is expected to grow exponentially by 2020.[36] According to the latest statistics, there are approximately 7.6 billion people in the world and growing.[37] Two in every three people in the world now have access to a portable mobile device. The ability to reach people instantly across anywhere in the world is no longer a sales and marketing dream, but an absolute reality. The physical barriers of time zones, distances, and countries no longer pose obstacles to reach target audiences.

Data analytics is the main tool for understanding how profile information from social media platforms is used. Data analytical tools more often focus on profile usage, sharing views, and engagement. Each interaction can be broken down even further to focus on the lowest level of interaction including: how many comments the user makes, volumetrics around the number of likes, shares and new followers, for example.

---

[36] GSMA Intelligence 2018, current year-end data except interpolated subscribers and connections https://bit.ly/2jcU6sS (Accessed 28/03/18).

[37] Current World Population https://bit.ly/Ism9T6 (Accessed 28/03/18).

Most social media platforms have their own data analytical tools to enable them to measure key performance indicators (KPIs). They are then able to choose from a variety of differing metrics. For example, Google Analytics focuses on gathering data from a wider range of information including interactions with third parties, desktop/mobile apps, and online shopping transactions. Twitter metrics also include the number of visits, followers, hashtag, URL link clicks, retweets, and total impressions on a profile.[38]

The growing impact of technology and its ability to process information (in as close to real time as possible) is putting increased burdens on companies. Given the rise in stricter data protection legislation with punitive financial penalties, pressure is on organizations to adapt and respond to data responsibilities quickly. Taking a practical and pragmatic approach to data governance is essential.

Stakeholders understanding the importance of data

There is the need for a variety of key stakeholders ranging across all levels and functions within the business. The

---

[38] Get Tweet engagement https://bit.ly/2qgOHH9 (Accessed 28/03/18).

Executive Board will need to effectively "sell" the benefits of data governance to any potential new board member.

Key executive supporters should be comprised of at least one or two board members (preferably from finance and operations). Financial backing is important to support the changes, as is operational buy-in to make amendments to existing processes. It is good to have as many supporters in your corner across the business, but the main thing is to secure senior level backing. Senior level backing in this sense means decision makers for the business.

Data governance is a combination of mapping business rules and standards, and measuring quality and identifying ownership at any given point of the data journey. Once the mapping is complete, the next step is to streamline them into a collective set that can be used throughout the organization. Having one set of data standards improves efficiency and quality as the organization is working to the same agreed set of rules.

Measuring quality is also about having the capability to track and quantify data at any given point. The way to measure quality is to compare the data in question against the business rules and data standards. Does the data comply with the standards? If not, identify and analyze the gaps. This continuous improvement approach to data will help ensure quality and accuracy are maintained.

The ability to identify who owns the data at any given time is important. Say for example, the same dataset is used multiple times by different parts of the business – who actually owns the data? In other words, if we can identify ownership, we are also able to identify accountability. New data technologies provide the capability to track data usage and if this means a wider group owns the data at different stages, then ultimately, they could all be accountable. Particularly with the introduction of new and stricter legislation, key stakeholders must understand their roles, responsibilities, and accountability with regards to handling data.

The message about data from top down (executive board to the workforce) to horizontally (between areas, functions, or groups) must be delivered clearly. The communication needs to make people aware of the importance of data usage and their accountability if anything potentially goes wrong. Once people are aware of the ramifications of the misuse of data, it then becomes important to explain how data governance can help to mitigate the risks of accountability through clearer communication, business rules, and data standards. With the entire organization now pointing in the same direction and using the same standardized sets of data, it becomes easier to identify ownership.

Underpinning data governance elements is the need for people within the organization to understand and support delivery of a data-driven approach. Data that is siloed off and not shared with other areas of the organization is at risk of not being governed at the enterprise level. If data is not managed from a centralized perspective, the siloes may be non-conformant with best practice. In other words, siloed data may be out of step with ungovernable data which presents a greater risk to the organization if not checked. When data is found not to meet the corporate data standards, then the relevant owners should be identified along with the data in question, to understand the gaps and ascertain what steps are needed to bring the data back into alignment.

Managing these types of actions is a good example of an issue discussed at a data governance board, committee, or work group. The point here is that data governance provides a more technical forum to discuss issues that might not necessarily make it to conventional executive boards. Indeed, the relationship between accountability and data has become increasingly blurred by the growing demand for information that can help secure a competitive advantage across most sectors.

Blockers as stakeholders

Although some stakeholders can be immensely helpful in providing clarity on current processes, there are some who unfortunately are not as forthcoming. These are often experts that are able to influence others because of their vast subject knowledge. In my experience, there is a myriad of challenges in getting these people on board. For example, powerful stakeholders don't have the time to engage properly because of other pressing commitments like running the company for example! Others resent having to engage at a lower level because it may be considered laborious, particularly if they feel their own time could be better used elsewhere more effectively.

So, we've also been able to identify the potential stakeholders who could be blockers in the change process. We've briefly examined some of the motivations for this type of behavior already. It's important to understand some of the rationale behind blocker behavior because we can then decide what type of mitigation to employ.

There are a variety of tactics deployed to tackle blockers. Understanding the blocker position and relative power within the organization is a fundamental part of intelligence gathering. The general questions are likely to be formed out of common sense. For example, do they hold influence at the senior level? Can you exert leverage with other colleagues or influence the wider group to share and support your point of view? In other words, are you able to persuade others by consensus? This is usually done by sticking to facts in a clear pragmatic way. Often the majority will take precedence and will take all views into account before arriving at a final decision.

The most important of all skills for a data architect, irrespective of domain or whether business, solution, data, or software areas, is communication. The ability to communicate in a way that your specific audience can understand is the most important tool required.

Then, there is a traditional approach of seeking a higher-level sponsor to facilitate a smoother passage for you. Going above, around or past the blocker to achieve your desired goal may be the better option. However, it also comes with risks. The first and most obvious risk is causing significant damage to the relationship with the blocker and their team. Burning bridges is an idiomatic expression, often used when there is no chance of recourse or further contact with a given relationship.

It is important to factor all potential risks when conducting preliminary and discovery work. Although you may not have all the views available, a stakeholder matrix tool will help to ensure there is a record of all your engagement across the business.

A stakeholder matrix is based on the seminal work of A. Mendelow.[39] In essence, Mendelow suggested the best way of capturing stakeholders was to place them in a grid according to their power and interest within the organization. The approach is relatively simple, which is

---

[39] Stakeholder Mapping; Mendelow, A.L.; Proceedings of the 2nd International Conference on Information Systems; Cambridge, MA; 1991.

why it remains effective today. There are four quadrants to the matrix:

1. High Power / Low Interest (Keep content) Directors, Executive Board Members	2. High Power / High Interest (Keep actively involved) Executive sponsors, Directors, project manager
3. Low Interest / Low Power (Monitor with minimal effort) Wider set of corporate stakeholders, customers, and data sharing partners	4. High Interest / Low Power (Keep constantly informed) Teams directly involved in data governance activity

- **Quadrant No 1: high power/low interest.** This group will usually be formed of senior stakeholders like Directors and Executive Board Members, and although they may not have a direct interest in your project, they are likely to wield considerable power. It is especially important to keep this group content.

- **Quadrant No 2: high power/high interest.** This group will usually be formed of senior sponsors at the Director, Executive Board, and Project Manager levels. This quadrant is your group of key supporters and will have a direct interest in your project. It is particularly important to keep this group closely involved in the project at all times.

- **Quadrant No 3: low interest/low power.** This group will usually be formed of a wider set of stakeholders who require monitoring with minimal effort. In other words, this quadrant is likely to have a passing interest in your work. Information passed to this group could be performed as part of wider corporate communication, without the need to inform directly.

- **Quadrant No 4: high interest/low power**. This group will usually be comprised of stakeholders who will be directly working within the project but will be reporting upwards to managers (likely to be those in Quadrant 2). This quadrant is likely to be directly involved in the daily activities of the project. Quadrant 4 group members include architects, project managers, business analysts, IT teams, and data subject matter experts.

The process for managing a stakeholder matrix is simple. The steps are set out as follows:

1. List all your stakeholders irrespective of power and interest.

2. Rank your stakeholders in order of priority, power, and interest.

3. Place your stakeholders in the appropriate quadrant.

4. Continuously manage the matrix to ensure all stakeholders are captured correctly as shifts occur in the power and interest categories.

A stakeholder matrix is a valuable tool to help map out the important stakeholders within the organization. As such, it is important to ensure that attention is given to all quadrants, as stakeholder dynamics, their interests, and relationships evolve constantly. In other words, it may be possible for stakeholders to move between quadrants frequently, so it is best to ensure the matrix is kept current.

Data governance questions

We now turn to challenging questions about data governance and IT systems more generally. Some may involve asking challenging questions to stakeholders across the business, others might require further reflection as the impact of new technologies on data governance are yet to emerge.

- What is a single version of the truth? This is not one of those big philosophical or existential questions; it is related to data integrity and quality. When information is received, how can we be sure of its accuracy and/or authenticity? Is there anything that can be done to mitigate the risks?

- How important is data to the organization? What are the business' strategic goals over the next five years and where does data fit within the plan?

- What does the current state of data look like? Is it fragmented, is it aligned, or is it siloed across ring fenced systems?

- Is there a need to migrate data to achieve better data management? Putting data into one place may help to drive out an end state of delivering greater analytics by clashing new combinations of datasets. This opens up further questions about technology choice and costings; a) is a data reservoir or data lake the preferred choice, b) is there a cheaper option available, c) is the latest technology really going to make a difference? If so, when will we see the benefits and a return on investment?

- If migration is not a viable option, then what else is out there? Could we deploy new technology development such as Application Program Interface (API) messaging or cloud-shared services to seek out data from existing stores and bring back to the center for analysis?

- Perhaps most importantly, is there an agreed definition of each data item across the business? The key to achieving data harmonization is to ensure that each business definition has its own unique data item definition. How can we achieve this? Using tools and methods like data dictionaries, data models, and specialized software to map out definitions can help. But also get the message out to key decision makers, using meetings, workshops, or internal media communications to ensure the widest possible coverage and agreement across the business.

Addressing the above set of questions is just one approach of many, towards achieving better data management. Each organization is likely to have a different response to the above questions and the ultimate challenge for any data person is to bring both business processes and data activity together in an aligned and understandable format.

"Data is the life blood of an organization or business" stated David Ellis in his opinion piece.[40] Ellis highlights the importance of protecting data by considering the need for secure backup in case of catastrophic failure. An organization without effective protection or data back-up, is taking a massive risk with its disaster recovery procedures. From a data governance perspective, the lack of disaster recovery would need to be addressed as a priority.

Let's return to the quest for a single version of the truth. Using a variety of the tools proposed above it is possible to reach that point of business and data alignment. The trick is to keep on top of constant change. To achieve this, the organization must be able to respond effectively. Having a

---

[40] Ellis, D; Data the Lifeblood of a Business; Computer Weekly; January 2014; https://bit.ly/2Ejmusz (Accessed 18/07/17).

data governance system fully operational provides the business with a deeper understanding of the impacts and requirements around data. A data governance system also provides the business with greater assurance when handling data-related matters such as regulation, transparency, and compliance.

About metadata

I often find the definition of metadata can cause fractious debate. Technical colleagues of mine often turn ashen and groan in agony when they hear those fateful words "metadata is data about data." Often this (now immortalized) phrase is used by those with a non-technical background. Why? Because it is simple to grasp and at the highest most abstract level possible; it is also correct.

Taking this one level down, metadata describes the physical characteristics of the data (such as format, length, and type). Why is metadata so important in data governance? Understanding how the physical components support the data itself allows us to repeat the same structural patterns for other data items. If all data items follow the same metadata structure or patterns, in theory you have then created a business data standard. Once a standard has been created and signed off by the business, it is then easier to monitor and apply control to new data items. A simple example is to imagine metadata is like the scaffolding of a building. Scaffolding looks to use common sized brackets, clamps, planks, and poles to support buildings. Using the standardized scaffolding enables you to predict how many specific items are required to support the building. Like scaffolding, metadata provides useful information to the data modeler or architect about the way a certain data item is constructed. Developing metadata standards that are flexible enough to cater for the "to be" world allow the business to ensure its data assets can keep up with the latest technology and development.

About blockchain

One reason behind the relative obscurity of blockchain is because it is the open source technology used to record Bitcoin (a digital cryptocurrency) transactions. Put simply, all data transactions are recorded in *blocks* using multiple servers and then a *chain* is created by circulating copies of the record across the network or Internet. Parts of the chain can then be checked for authenticity.

The reason why blockchain is considered secure is because it requires a twofold approach to breach: 1) access to all servers that have copies of the transaction, and 2) access to all servers and performed at the same time. Blockchain is not just for banking-related data, it can potentially be used for other sensitive data such as medical or tax information.

Blockchain uses peer to peer (P2P) networks, so users effectively allow their computers to become nodes across a larger network. A larger network allows for greater bandwidth and facilitates larger data sharing to occur. When conducted over the Internet, digital transactions using blockchain are open source and therefore access to records tend to be cheaper than accessing existing data stores. Again, being on a P2P network, the emphasis is on self-regulation and governance.

From a data governance point of view, the fact that blockchain is self-regulated and open-source means that most digital transactions are based on trust and relationships. In some ways this is a positive step and a data governance system could help support the way that transactions are conducted by an organization. In other words, a business using blockchain would have clear guidance and documentation provided to ensure every transaction was managed in the same uniformed manner.

In conclusion, blockchain is likely to be a watching brief for many organizations, as the capabilities of this technology are only beginning to unfold. Having a data governance system already in place provides the organization with greater assurance to test disruptive technologies as they emerge and ensure the integrity of its data assets remains intact.

CHAPTER 6

D474: A Case Study

D474 is our fictional company we are using to illustrate the key concepts that have been discussed in earlier chapters. The scenarios presented here are based upon real-life examples and situations surrounding data governance. The rationale for pulling these scenarios together as a fictional case study is to make the point that data governance is bespoke to your organization. In other words, data governance is not a "one size fits all" system. The objective is to take what works best for you and adapt into your organization.

There are two different D474 scenarios presented. Scenario 1 looks at the initial rationale for creating a data governance system. This includes looking at the essential components needed to make data governance effective. Scenario 2 looks at a practical example of data governance in action. Here there is a change to legislation and D474 needs to alter its systems or risk becoming non-compliant.

D474 Scenario 1 – creating a data governance system

Our fictional company, D474 understands that data is important but now recognizes the wider business opportunities available. Data can help bring D474 and its customers closer together. If D474 can provide a personalized service through new data analytical insight into its customer profiles, there is greater chance of sustaining the customer relationship over a longer term.

In terms of organizational structure, D474 has a centralized policy-making function, which was created to manage compliance/regulatory issues on behalf of the business. Areas such as operations, marketing, legal, compliance, and HR, have evolved over time and developed their own data management practices. These data practices are siloed and there is no coordination across the business.

D474 has built up a good relationship with policy functions within the business but has not gone beyond this with other stakeholders. The central policy function did not need to engage with any other area to fulfil its requirements. Other business functions usually interact with operations, since they are more closely aligned. However, the constant growth of data across all business areas has resulted in the need to create a coordinated data function.

D474 want to expand business opportunities by exploiting its customer base. However, D474 has no coordinated approach to manage its data assets effectively. To achieve its goals, D474 needs to build a centralized data governance function. For the purposes of Executive Board approval, the benefits of data governance transformation for D474 are set out below.

Defining D474's data governance benefits

Data governance as a function sets the strategic direction for data by:

- aligning to the strategic business of D474 (using richer data to understand customers);

- shifting organizational behavior from silo-related data functions to D474 enterprise data;

- developing robust common data standards for the business to ensure D474 is compliant with global regulatory standards as and when they emerge;

- informing policy change through a data quality service that is responsive and flexible to change;

- ensuring data standards are managed, enforced, and periodically reviewed to ensure they remain fit for purpose and deliver consistency throughout;

- driving up quality and value through streamlined data quality and data acquisition services for the business;

- providing integrity assurance and enforcement of the above through clear data governance and accountability across the business;

- mitigating Executive Board risks by exploiting data in more effective ways including supporting technical solutions that drive up the business's analytical capabilities; and

- articulating the benefits of having richer data across the business including greater assurance and for data disclosure providing informed policy-making for the business; and building a stronger reputation across industry by sharing data with more confidence.

Mapping out the benefits in this way helps D474 understand why creating a data governance function is important. It is also important to show how data governance can help to deliver D474's strategic vision.

Data governance aligns to D474's strategic vision

The data governance function is responsible for delivering changes to how D474 manages data and aligns to the strategic business vision. D474's strategic vision will be aligned to maximizing profits within greater efficiency. For D474, data governance functionality will mean using information systems to better understand its customer needs. Harnessing this information into better analytical output will help generate better product development and ensure customer demands are being met at the right place and right time.

As part of transformation, D474 will be driving awareness across the business and acknowledging data as a corporate and valuable strategic asset. Aligned to this recognition are wider impacts of exploiting richer data to identify new product and service opportunities and develop stronger customer relationships in as close to as real time.

The impact of these changes will be experienced across the whole of the business. D474's data governance team will deliver its objectives through the newly established strands, including data architecture, data acquisition, data quality, and data standards, either by direct engagement with specific project management delivery programs or each line of business. These groups are known as (internal) key stakeholders. Examples of these key stakeholders include lines of business, the IT team, and the Finance and Executive Board.

D474's data governance team will work with all stakeholders to build understanding and seek agreement that future data usage incorporates the common agreed principles as set out in data policy. The objective is for data governance to be collaboratively working with policymakers at the conceptual stage of policy design. The benefits of this approach are to embed the principle that data is a strategic asset of value and clearly understand what outcomes are achievable within expected timelines.

Moving from siloed behaviors to enterprise data for the D474 business

Moving from siloed behaviors to an organizational-driven approach is a key priority for D474 transformation. With regards to D474, it is helpful that established working relationships exist between business areas. Applying data governance to mature business areas helps smooth the way when introducing data standards, the use of third party information, and sharing information with other companies.

Through ownership of data standards, the D474 data governance team will play an important strategic role in ensuring transformation programs embed the common standard for data approach across the business. The IT department, as provider of technical solutions, is another key stakeholder in ensuring the organization can benefit from cleaner data.

Ensuring data governance drives the policy of D474 data

From a data governance perspective, the purpose of data policy is to strategically inform the governance, acquisition, ingestion, transformation, and analytical use of information which is under the control of the business. The impact of data means data governance will be a key driver across the business working with key stakeholders to develop data policy that is aligned to strategic business priorities and senior management commitments. The remit of data governance is wide-ranging. It is important that governance and policies are sufficiently robust to realize the strategic vision of transformation into a richer data-driven organization.

There is a close interdependency between policy and strategy. However, the key objective is for data governance to establish a clear set of data controls, guidelines and rules that are underpinned by policies that champion all data as a valuable asset for the business.

Informing D474 policy change through data quality

There is likely to be a transitional period when dealing with data quality across D474 legacy systems and these issues will be identified via the data quality service. D474's data quality service will look at handling data inconsistencies as soon as they arise. The tactical solution might be to cleanse the data. Depending on the degree of issue, the service will look to resolve or escalate upwards to the data governance board for a steer or decision.

Any findings from commissioned work (such as "data journeys" that map out the end-to-end processes) will also be escalated via the data quality service on to the Data Governance Board, which will act as final decision-making authority on funding or issues of contentious / sensitive nature.

It is accepted there are challenges with data quality across the organization. Some of these issues are being discussed at working level through business area workshops – for example Master Data Management solutions and ensuring all external information coming into the organization meets agreed data standards, so that it is appropriately formatted and provides more informed analysis.

Without clear and effective management of your data and data quality, you're facing several risks that may include:

Risks	Mitigation
Lack of executive management control and review around data usage.	Embedding data governance principles across the business by championing an internal communications campaign on data governance.
Poor quality, inaccurate and untimely data within organization.	Data Quality Service working with Business to scrub data in short term. Seek to identify root cause of data quality, internal or at front door? Does it require physical system or higher-level policy change?
Third party information data not formatted correctly for business purposes.	Publication of Data Standards endorsing and advising approach for all incoming data to be transmitted in a common way. Physical solution may also involve introducing new technologies such as application program interface (APIs) to improve data sharing capability with external parties.
Is data of enough quality to meet statutory financial and reporting requirements?	Working with key stakeholders across the business to ensure relevant data feeds and data standards meet any existing criteria / accreditation.

The D474 Data Quality Service is likely to highlight and escalate issues using a twin track approach. In part, by data scrubbing, this will hopefully provide a short-term remedial fix. The second part of data quality will look to identify root causes which are more likely to require a permanent fix through a combination of business change, policy, and/or legislation. By data scrubbing in the short term, there is an opportunity for data quality to inform the need for policy change benefitting the wider business in the longer term.

Developing and delivery of common data standards for the D474 business

The development of common data standards is a useful tool in helping to define wider opportunities for the business. For example, the use of common D474 data standards is a key factor in determining the quality and accuracy of third party information. The D474 data standards need to be defined enough to meet current relegation for compliance purposes. They also need to be flexible enough to meet new international standards as they emerge. Although these issues are all under consideration in the wider transformation arena, it is important to continually review data standards so they are fit for purpose and responsive enough to adapt to change.

Ensuring D474 data standards are managed, enforced, and continuously reviewed

This continuous approach towards data standards is necessary as the business moves through the gears and levels of implementation. Data standards are effective markers to help the business ensure future data is captured and recorded in a common and agreed manner.

Driving up quality and value through streamlined data quality and data acquisition services for the D474 business

There is an interwoven relationship between data acquisition and data quality. The objective is to ensure D474 delivers one streamlined data acquisition service which manages the end-to-end process on behalf of the business. Upon review, there were different stakeholders across the chain of activity that includes business case-led demand, supplier selection and acquisition, storage management, transformation, and resulting end user analytical capability. Bringing the different D474 actors together required a deeper review understand the issues and challenges facing each area. Understanding the current state allowed D474 to address by mapping resolutions against business concerns into the data governance transition plan. Transitioning into one streamlined service for data acquisition helped provide value and drive up quality assurance for data coming into the business, using commonly agreed data standards and clear governance. By centralizing the finances for data acquisition, it also meant that D474 costs were further reduced and financial controls were easier to manage.

Providing integrity assurance and enforcement through clear data governance and accountability across the business

Assuring the integrity of data that we hold is a vital component of the D474 data quality service but will also touch upon the internal controls the business places upon it. The D474 data governance function will use the data standards as a template and work with the business to build risk management controls upon the data received, stored, transformed, and utilized.

Separately working with Finance, Legal, and Operational teams across D474, the objective is to produce clearer governance and accountability around data users and data ownership. The data quality service will look to collaborate closely with the legal team to ensure any new data legislation is followed in a practical and compliance sense.

Mitigating strategic risks by exploiting data in more effective ways

The need to exploit data more effectively is a strategic ambition of the D474 executive board. We know that technologies such as data marts, lakes and cloud services are being considered as options for investment. Evaluating such technology is important to determine the best fit for D474 as a company.

Linked to data acquisition, is a need to better understand storage technologies to help D474 make informed decisions on the risks around data prioritization, storage, and access for predictive analytical use. D474 data governance will look at solutions that can handle multiple formats and transform data that can be handled effectively by new or existing systems. This includes supporting technical solutions that drive up D474's analytical capabilities.

Clearly articulating the benefits of having richer data across the D474 business

Using the data standards as the portal to allow or reject information, the benefits of richer data include an improvement in data quality, the ability to have greater confidence in the use of data for compliance and risk activity, and the capacity to analyze larger scale datasets across a broader range of variables.

Having set out the benefits for a data governance function above, the D474 executive board decides to accept and implement the recommendations. The objective is to implement a centralized function that will manage all data governance related issues on behalf of D474. As D474 begins to adopt all processes described above, the organization can begin to see benefits of improved data asset management by introducing a centralized data governance function.

The D474 transition to a centralized data governance function.

Before:

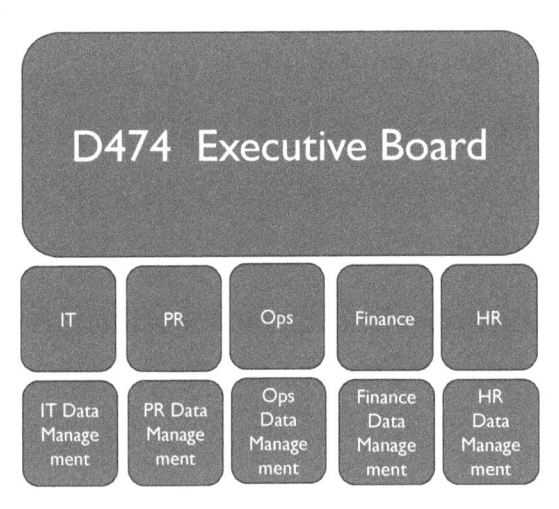

```
┌─────────────────────────────────────┐
│                                     │
│        D474  Executive Board        │
│                                     │
└─────────────────────────────────────┘
    ┌───┐  ┌───┐  ┌───┐  ┌─────┐  ┌───┐
    │IT │  │PR │  │Ops│  │Finance│ │HR │
    └───┘  └───┘  └───┘  └─────┘  └───┘
    ┌────┐ ┌────┐ ┌────┐ ┌──────┐ ┌────┐
    │ IT │ │ PR │ │Ops │ │Finance│ │ HR │
    │Data│ │Data│ │Data│ │ Data  │ │Data│
    │Mgmt│ │Mgmt│ │Mgmt│ │ Mgmt  │ │Mgmt│
    └────┘ └────┘ └────┘ └──────┘ └────┘
```

After:

```
                    D474  Executive Board
        IT      PR       Ops      Finance    HR
                      Data Governance
```

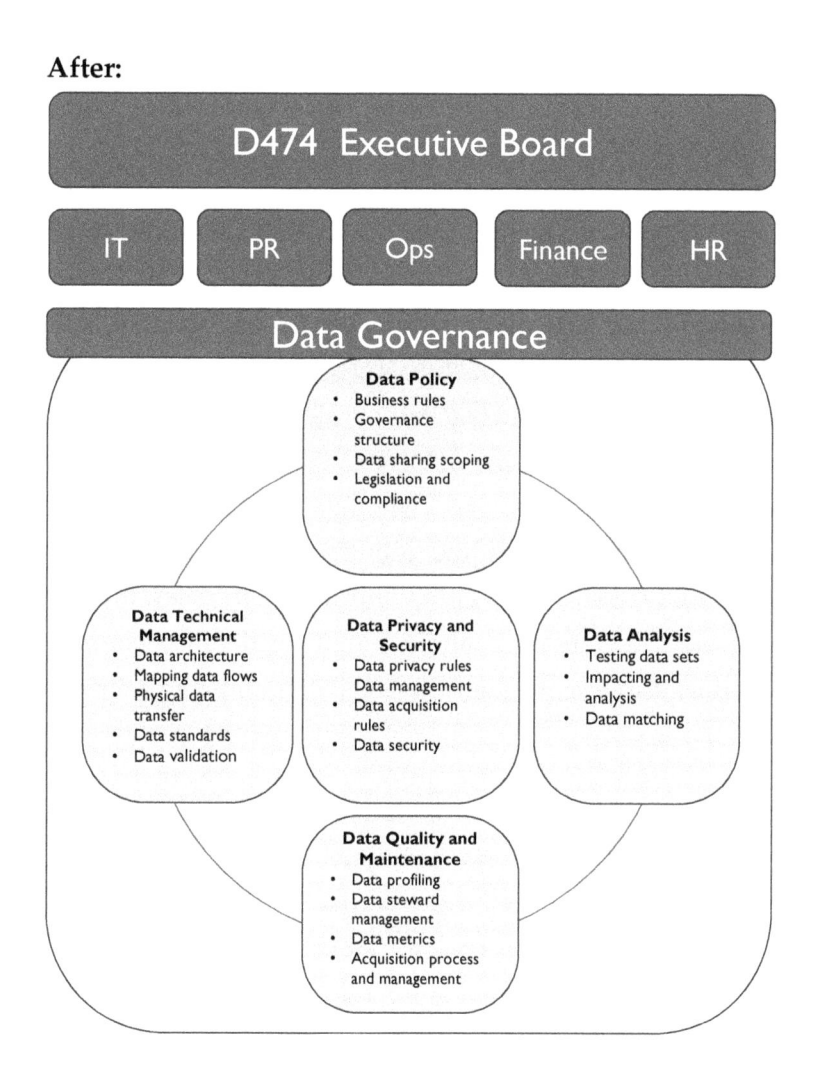

- **Data Policy**
  - Business rules
  - Governance structure
  - Data sharing scoping
  - Legislation and compliance

- **Data Technical Management**
  - Data architecture
  - Mapping data flows
  - Physical data transfer
  - Data standards
  - Data validation

- **Data Privacy and Security**
  - Data privacy rules
  - Data management
  - Data acquisition rules
  - Data security

- **Data Analysis**
  - Testing data sets
  - Impacting and analysis
  - Data matching

- **Data Quality and Maintenance**
  - Data profiling
  - Data steward management
  - Data metrics
  - Acquisition process and management

Scenario 2: D474 data governance in action

This example illustrates the data governance function can respond effectively to a change in legal requirements.

Here, a recent legislative change requires D474 to ensure it only retains customer data for a maximum of three months.

From a policy perspective, this will require some adjustment in terms of guidance and procedural overview. Inevitably the guidance will need to be updated and people across the organization must be made aware of the changes. How will this legislative change impact the D474 business in terms of productivity and effectiveness? The underlying question is whether storing customer information for only three months will affect business profitability. Still under policy but taking the view from a compliance perspective, there might need to be controls introduced to ensure the new legislation is being adhered to.

The bottom line for policy is that D474 must comply with the new regulations or risk being penalized. From a public relations perspective, the media fallout from non-compliance could be a risk not worth contemplating. The negative publicity could cause damage to D474's image and goodwill it has accrued over the years. The potential damage to reputation across the industry will result in financial loss in terms of customer business. In simple terms, being non-compliant is a scenario that should be avoided at all costs.

With the risk of potential catastrophic consequences in mind, often the tone of communication between policy and the delivery arms of the organization can be firm. For example, policy may stress the urgency of adhering to new legislation without necessarily providing the rationale or context. Issuing a "directive" is a process that has no real meaning unless the background behind the decision is provided.

Returning to the D474 brief, we know that the data policy team has established a compliance requirement to ensure systems do not hold customer data for longer than three months. After passing through data policy, the requirement is now passed to the IT architect to deliver a solution and a project manager is also assigned. But what roles do they play and how are they supposed to work together?

Understanding the roles that different D474 actors play

We now have three different D474 actors at play in this scenario: the IT enterprise architect, the project manager, and the policy/business operations lead. All these D474 actors have a critical role to play in ensuring business requirements are finalized and agreed with by key stakeholders. The requirements must also align with organizational strategy. The policy lead is likely to drive this phase as they will understand the current model and gaps that could be integrated into the new process.

The D474 architect will be looking at both strategic and systems-related developments. The questions likely to arise are: Do we have systems in place to deliver these changes. If not, what is needed to realize the business goal? Can we reuse existing components or is it a case of build or buy a packaged solution off the shelf? From a data perspective, how will the information be captured, stored, and accessed? Will it adhere to existing data standards or will the business need to create a new repository?

As these questions start to generate more discussion, the role of the D474 project manager is to capture these ideas and filter these into projects, milestones, and agreed deliverables. Perhaps this is the most challenging role, as it requires the project manager to ensure they fully understand what the project is delivering and for what purpose. Even though the role of project manager is working at the day-to-day level of implementation, it is important that they understand the strategic connections that sit above any one particular project. In some ways the D474 project manager role is to bring both policy and business operations leads and architect together. The second (and arguably most crucial) part of the role is to ensure the proposed IT solution fully meets the business requirements and is delivered on time.

From a strategic perspective, understanding the overarching business rationale is a common principle that all actors must agree upon. Otherwise, there is a risk of delivering a project that doesn't meet business requirements or expectations. In most cases there are clear demarcations between the roles. However, in practical terms, there have been instances where these roles overlap, and it can be difficult understanding who in D474 is responsible for delivering what.

For example, data analysis on the use of D474 customer information may be directly linked to sales. Here normal practices may include data scientists slicing and splicing datasets in different ways to test and validate sales information. This may mean using a variety of approaches to acquire, interrogate, and transform the data. If the datasets are unexpectedly larger than expected or data analysis processes are time consuming or repetitive, a potential solution might be to use AI or machine learning technology as a way of saving time.

This is where clear communication and agreement is required at the very start of the process to ensure D474 teams understand what they will be expected to deliver and to what timescale. What is certain is that a good D474 project manager will use tried and tested controls to drive a project through to completion. For example, tools such as weekly checkpoints, project plans, and timelines will help to ensure delivery remains on track.

In terms of core assumptions, we know what the business requirements are. Moving down towards the logical and physical layers, there needs to be an assessment made on the impact to systems and overall capacity. The D474 architect alongside the project and business managers would consider functional and nonfunctional requirements. In terms of distinguishing between the two, I find it is easier to think of user and business must haves as nonfunctional requirements and system needs as functional requirements.

Working collaboratively also means bringing D474 DevOps colleagues into conversations early. Here, adopting the Agile approach can be helpful in bringing teams together quickly. It may be tempting to get caught up in the interesting terminology of stand-up (the subject matter expert at the time will lead the group and stand down when the project moves on in development) and sprints (developing ideas at speed, so if they fail, they do faster and give the project time to focus on alternatives). The underlying point is to ensure that you have all the experts providing input at the right time.

In this scenario, we know that the D474 business requirement is to delete customer data after three months. This is a nonfunctional requirement. The system change that may be required, for example putting a flag in the IT system and purging the data repository every three months, is a functional requirement.

In terms of functional requirements, it could also be a case of applying date and time filters on the existing system to isolate customer datasets that are close to the 3-month deadline. Filtering datasets and placing them in a separate environment provides an opportunity to interrogate data before deletion. The process of deletion might also be automated. This would need a clear process control mechanism in place to ensure the correct data is being deleted when and where appropriate. In terms of process, we know there are date filters set just before the 3-month window.

Here, there is an opportunity for the D474 data steward to define the process clearly. The business needs at least two full weeks to analyze and filter datasets before deletion, so in recognizing the demands and pressures across D474, the data steward would work with the data scientists to map together a process that would enable the isolation, interrogation, and analysis of any customer-related data before deletion.

A simplified monthly cycle of handling customer data is shown below:

Week 1
- Ensure customer data is accurate and amend if necessary.
- Any amendments must require sign-off from the business lead and data steward.

- Test AI and storage environment capability with "dummy data" before live data scenarios.

Week 2
- Use Date Filters to isolate customer data and move to separate environment.
- Grant data scientists access to isolated data to perform analytics.
- Scientists identify any variances or issues and notify stewards and the business lead.

Week 3
- Scientists compile a report with recommendations for stewards and the business lead. Any major issues are escalated upwards for Data Governance Board to make a decision.
- Board makes decision.
- Business steward takes remedial action.

Week 4
- Customer data is deleted.
- Compliance reports are generated to demonstrate adherence to policy and regulations.

Mapping a process is usually the domain of project managers, but the D474 data steward would have an important role in ensuring all areas of the business understand and agree to the process. This process control mechanism would also be approved by the Data Governance Board. The main reason for escalation to the

D474 Board is simply to ensure everyone has oversight and agrees to the proposed approach.

Of course, there are multiple permutations depending on the form of data governance your own organization has in place. Whatever the configuration might be, the core functions of governance, development, and implementation will still be present. If these functions are not available, then a data governance system would soon identify and escalate these process gaps as a risk.

As we move lower into the infrastructure of the D474 systems, we then begin to ask questions about capability, functionality, and deliverability. This is the realm of D474 Dev/Ops or solution architects and they will be able to provide guidance on questions such as:

- *Are systems able to handle change?* For D474, we will say "yes." The existing systems can apply filters to extract, analyze, and delete the relevant data.

- *Storage and retention?* Here, we are aware D474 has created a separate environment to isolate and analyze the data before it is deleted in accordance with new regulations. In terms of data retention, this is only for a short period of time and there is a transparent process in place.

- *Reuse, build, or buy?* Whenever considering a system change, the three architectural pillars (reuse, build, or buy) are always considered. This question of which pillar D474 should stand by is not just for solution architects; it is a wider question for the business. The fundamental issue is whether a new system meets all D474 business requirements. The second issue is given the potential cost involved, how long would a return on investment materialize? In other words, is it economically viable for D474 to invest in a new system? For example, a new D474 enterprise reporting system could be implemented which would require all areas of the business to provide returns monthly. This would allow D474 management to analyze returns and ensure compliance or be able to address issues of non-compliance found. Likewise, if guidance for such a system is media-based and accessible via the intranet, then updating information could be simplified via an off-the-shelf content management system or reusing something that already exists within D474's systems.

From a D474 data governance perspective, it is fundamentally important to ensure the functions behind data usage are managed with care and precision. Like the implementation of a new IT system, the best way to check whether data governance works is to monitor and report monthly. As set out above, D474's creation of a new executive board chaired by the new Data Director will help to ensure that data-related matters are managed across the organization effectively.

The most practical and arguably most simple approaches to manage the transition are:

- **Slow phased.** Organizations will need to evaluate which area needs development first. The creation of a data policy function for example may be a greater priority for organizations that do not have existing policy-making controls in place. In this phase, transition is gradual and the dependencies on existing processes to meet new demands intensify. Here, existing systems are being asked to manage new processes. The risk is that new data demands may be out of scope of current systems, so the transition process needs to be managed carefully. The reason why existing systems or processes cannot cope with change is simply because they are not designed for additional services. Therefore, legacy systems generally come under greater scrutiny because of their perceived lack of capability. One might argue that legacy systems were built for a specific requirement and therefore delivered accordingly at the time. Adding new processes to legacy processes may risk overburdening the entire system. With this in mind, a slow transition is required. In this sense, taking an enterprise level or horizontal view across the IT landscape becomes more challenging as different systems have evolved at different times. This approach is likely to be favored by large organizations with many legacy systems that have grown independently of one another.

- **Medium phased.** Introduce new systems and processes into the organization as soon are they are ready to be delivered. Here the approach would be like a waterfall software development lifestyle technique. In other words, each stage of development would have to be approved by the Data Governance Board. As each phase is deployed, there is a degree of parallel running with both old and new processes operational at the same time. As the new process is embedded, the legacy system is phased out over a period. The length of duration required to switch over from one set of processes to another will be dependent on timing, size, and complexity. Timing is about when is the best time for the business to initiate a switch over to the new process? An organization's size is a key factor in establishing whether it is flexible enough to cope with a sudden or gradual implementation. The general rule is the larger the organization, the longer it will take to change direction. Complexity in terms of business processes, is an issue that is often considered at the earliest stages of new development. Indeed, there is also a tendency to assume that an IT solution will resolve these issues.

However, while an IT "fix" might seem appealing to the organization, it may not resolve the root cause of the issue. It is important to first understand why the problem is arising in the first place. Quite simply, a rethink on the existing system is required. It may be that a new business process is required, and an IT solution can help improve efficiency.

- **Fast phased**. There are two approaches. Those organizations which have stable policy-making areas may be able to incorporate data governance functions into existing processes. This approach is arguably the most seamless and easiest way to incorporate new governance. By expanding existing functionality to accommodate new controls and processes, or put another way, running parallel systems of old and new will help to establish which controls can be turned off or decommissioned quickly. The "big bang" approach stops existing practices immediately and adopts the new model of data governance right away. This method is effectively "performing open heart surgery" on the organization, as quickly changing to a new system and discarding the old infrastructure may leave severe repercussions. Indeed, the new approach may get rejected because the organization is not able to cope with such drastic change in one go.

However, if the organization is relatively small, it may be easier to adjust.

Based on what we know about D474 so far, the transition path is likely to be slow phased at first in order to manage the change. Once the overarching data governance structure is in place, D474 will be in a stronger position to manage a medium to fast phased data transition more effectively.

The above is a very brief run through a typical example of the sorts of issues an organization is likely to face when dealing with data. The main objective is to illustrate the myriad of issues that may arise.

In conclusion, we have run through an end-to-end solution to illustrate how a requirement might be managed. Starting from data policy analysis, the requirement passes through businesses, project, and architecture hands, before moving to the DevOps team. It is important to ensure that all relevant actors are brought into the project lifecycle at the right time. The project manager should ensure that all relevant stakeholders are involved and kept informed of progress.

While the solution requires a recording of dates within the existing system, it is important to go through the above sequence of data governance processes for consistency and to ensure D474 systems remain effective in handling data.

Developing data management tools for D474

The next section pulls together data management tools or (artifacts) that are needed to build a data governance model. These include a stakeholder matrix used to identify relationships and rank levels of influence.

D474 Stakeholder Matrix

A stakeholder matrix, as first explained earlier, is a useful tool to help map out the important stakeholders within the organization. It is important to ensure that attention is given to all quadrants since stakeholder dynamics, interests, and relationships evolve constantly. It may be possible for stakeholders to move between quadrants frequently, so it is best to ensure the matrix is updated regularly. Here is it again for us to review.

1. High Power / Low Interest (Keep content) Directors, Executive Board Members	2. High Power / High Interest (Keep actively involved) Executive sponsors, Directors, project manager
3. Low Interest / Low Power (Monitor with minimal effort) Wider set of corporate stakeholders, customers, and data sharing partners	4. High Interest / Low Power (Keep constantly informed) Teams directly involved in data governance activity

It is important to note that stakeholders on the matrix can move between quadrants at any time.

For example, customers and data sharing partners are captured as 3 interest/low power above, but this would change to 2 high power/high interest, if the focus was on data sharing.

D474 Data governance board template

The next tool is the template for D474's data governance board. Establishing a data governance board sends a positive statement that D474 is ready to transform to a data-driven enterprise. The template is communicated across D474 to ensure greater visibility and impact. Defining the data function, its role and responsibilities ensure greater understanding of data governance across D474.

D474 DATA GOVERNANCE BOARD

1 Purpose

1.1 The D474 Data Governance Board is responsible for ensuring that data governance is embedded in the organization and that legislation and all data standards are met.

1.2 It will also provide assurance to the D474 Executive Board of Directors that the organization has effective systems of internal control in relation to risk management and data governance.

2. Accountability

2.1 The D474 Data Governance Board is accountable to and will report directly to the D474 Executive Board of Directors.

3. Membership

3.1 The Data Governance Committee shall be appointed by the D474 Executive Board of Directors.

3.2 The D474 Data Governance Board membership shall consist of:

- A Non-Executive Chairman or Director – appointed by the D474 Board of Directors.

- At least 1 Nonexecutive Deputy Director – appointed by the D474 Board of Directors who shall act as a deputy when required.

- Chairpersons of all reporting D474 working groups from Data Quality, Data Acquisition, Data Policy, and Data Engineering.

- Other attendees may include the Director of Finance, Business Development Manager, Chief Operating Officer, and Director of HR.

- Any standing member of D474's Executive Board of Directors

A nominated deputy may attend in the absence of any of the above.

3.3 The D474 Executive Board of Directors will review membership of the Data Governance Board annually to ensure that it best reflects the requirements of governance across the organization.

3.4 The Chairperson of the D474 Data Governance Board will serve for up to two years. Nonexecutive members will serve for up to two years and be eligible for reappointment for a further two years, if deemed appropriate by the Data Governance Board.

4. Administration

4.1 The Data Governance Board shall appoint a Secretariat to prepare agendas, keep minutes, and handle other matters concerning the administration of the Committee.

4.2 Reports from the reporting working groups will be provided to the Data Governance Board in advance of any Board meeting. The chairpersons of the data working groups should ensure that any relevant report has been sent to the Data Governance Board Secretariat or advise that the working group has not met.

4.3 Any member of staff may raise an issue with the Chairman by written submission. The Chairman will decide whether the issue shall be included in the Committee's business. The individual raising the matter may be invited to attend.

5. Frequency of meetings

5.1 Meetings will be held no less than four times in each financial reporting year.

5.2 The Data Governance Board may require the attendance of any director, or member of staff, and the production of any document it considers relevant to data governance or related activities.

5.3 Impromptu meetings may be called at the request of any three members of the Data Governance Board or the Chairman of the D474 Board of Directors.

6. Quorum

6.1 A quorum will consist of not fewer than four members of the Data Governance Board with at least the following members present:

- The Data Governance Chairperson or Deputy, one of whom should chair the meeting.

- The Chairpersons or Deputies from the reporting Data Working Groups so each group is represented.

6.2 A record of attendance will be maintained and made available for audit or reporting requirements.

7. Duties and responsibilities

7.1 To provide regular reports to the D474 Board of Directors on significant issues or concerns. This will be in the form of exceptional escalated issues arising at the Data Governance Board. The minutes of the Data Governance Board will be presented to the D474 Executive Board of Directors. If required, quarterly reports on key issues will also be made available. If required, Data Governance Board minutes will be made available for audit purposes.

7.2 To receive reports which identify new areas of legislation, policy, or other requirements with which D474 is required to comply, together with an assessment of the organization's ability to meet the new requirements, and any further action required.

7.3 To receive detailed reports from the working groups which highlight progress against quality targets and plans, and areas of underperformance in any aspect of data quality or customer service.

7.4 Review any risk registers and/or action plans ensuring that up-to-date information is available.

7.5 Monitor and support collaboration with other working groups, operational areas, customers, and public.

7.6 Ensure that equality and diversity principles underpin all data-related functions and strategies related to all areas of D474 activity.

7.7 The Data Governance Board will ensure robust improvement plans are put in place to address performance concerns and will ensure the D474 Executive Board is made aware of significant areas of concern.

8. Board member responsibilities

8.1 The following list is not exhaustive, but is used to illustrate the responsibilities and behaviors required:

- Understand the responsibilities of their role as a Data Governance Board Member.

- Understand and comply with the D474's strategic vision and mandate related to data.

- Ensure D474 as the organization pursues its purpose (as defined in the governing document).

- Safeguard the name, values, and goodwill of D474 and make decisions as a collective body.

- Understand the role and delegated authority of any working groups.

- Hold meetings as often and when necessary to properly discharge their duties ethically as a Board Member.

- Understand D474's legal structure and position on data-related matters.

- Manage conflicts of interest across D474 as the organization.

- Provide strategic and financial oversight and ensure that resources are managed effectively.

- Ensure that all potential data risks are assessed and managed with due care and attention in accordance with relevant legislation.

- Seek expert and professional advice on data-related matters when required.

9 Monitoring board effectiveness

9.1 The Data Governance Board will monitor its effectiveness by reviewing its responsibilities by reporting to the D474 Executive Board on a quarterly basis.

10. Review

10.1 The Data Governance Board will review the Terms of Reference on an annual basis to ensure it remains relevant and fit for purpose.

10.2 The Data Governance Board will also conduct an annual assessment to establish whether it remains suitable to discharge a data governance functions and duties on behalf of D474.

Developing data principles for D474: A closer review

This section looks at developing data principles for D474. The approach uses a specific set of questions to refine principles to become specific and relevant for D474 data governance.

> Data governance for D474 will incorporate capture, store, retain, and manage data for the benefit of the organization.

What is the principle? Here at first glance, the statement is about the process for capturing and storing data. If you look closer, the addition of organizational benefit goes beyond a specific process or event. There are many possibilities or interpretations of the term *benefit of the organization*. However, not being specific is the aim. Having abstract statements provides the opportunity to capture as many different scenarios as possible.

Why is this principle a potential problem? Here, you should be thinking about summarizing the concern, concept, or issue.

Before we do this, it's worth making a point when highlighting issues. You may find dismissing a principle easier, rather than see the potential benefits. It may be valuable to apply a health warning over this step. Be critical, but not at the expense of creativity. The purpose of this step is to test whether a principle is robust enough to stand up to intensive scrutiny. Complete destruction will be counterproductive and likely result in staggered process. A wise person once said to me, "It is better to run with an idea than with none at all!" In some ways even if an idea or a concept fails early, it helps the business find an alternative solution quicker and more effectively.

Turning to the data principle in question, we can see there may be some concern about the statement. Ask the question, is the capture, storage, and retention of data really an issue? Why? Has the reason been articulated effectively? We know that D474's concern is about the many ways it is potentially storing the same set of information. There are no effective controls and therefore no way to manage quality or process. The rather obvious intention is the inclusion of the now familiar term *benefit of the organization.* Putting a positive spin implies that some action will be taken to address the issue.

How will you address the issue?

As mentioned earlier, the principle should be able to summarize the process or activity undertaken to resolve or mitigate. Looking closer, the principle does not cover *how* data will be captured and stored in the future.

So, the principle could be amended as follows:

> Capture, store, retain, and manage data *using relevant technology for* the benefit of the organization (setting scope).

We can now see that D474 will resolve its data management issues using relevant technology. Obviously, this is still very high level, but it at least enables the reader to understand the approach or next steps anticipated. There is enough scope to allow for a few technology options, hence the use of the term *relevant*. It could be, in fact, that existing technology is more than able to meet the business requirement. In other words, "If it ain't broke, don't fix it!"

This might be painful to hear for new technology suppliers or management consultants for example, but for the D474 Finance department this is likely to be a sweet melody. There is the perpetual drive to seek balance between existing and new technologies. For D474, it is about meeting demand but using existing technology wherever possible. This leads us quite neatly to the final step in evaluating a principle.

What is the intended outcome? Here, the principle should be able to describe the result and benefit of these actions. In this case, D474's need for improved data governance is captured as a benefit. We are then indicating that after some form of action or intervention has taken place, this will be a positive result or beneficial for the business. It may be considered optimistic in some quarters to suggest that an action (that hasn't been expressly documented) will result in a beneficial outcome for the organization. So be prepared for challenge from corners that might be more skeptical.

So, after going through the steps, we have now made a few amendments to the principle. It now reads as data governance for D474 will:

> Capture, store, retain, and manage data *using relevant technology for* the benefit of D474 as an organization.

Let's review the next drafted D474 principle which states:

> Use of technology and tools to maintain highest standards of quality (use of data analytics, cleansing and profiling) to deliver accurate and confident data.

Adopting the same approach and going through the steps will help test whether this principle meets the business objective or requirement.

What is the principle? Here, it is important to think about a specific issue or title. We know this is about technology and its use. The aim is clearly stated.

Why is this principle a potential problem? Here, you should be thinking about summarizing the concern, concept, or issue. The principle mentions the use of technology and tools. What exactly are these for D474? It is fairly abstract. Do we know *why* this is the chosen approach? Technology is merely one way of delivering a solution for D474. It is not the only way. And as we already know, much of technology success is dependent upon how the solution meets the business requirements set. Turning back to the principle itself, we know that the potential choice of technology could be an issue if it cannot deliver what D474 expects it to.

How will you address the issue? Here, the principle should be able to summarize the process or activity undertaken to resolve or mitigate. The principle then moves on to address the D474 concern by using data analytics, cleansing, and profiling. Why have these activities been selected ahead of others? These are specific data-related activities and perhaps may be considered too low level. However, they do illustrate the kinds of activity required for D474, so it may be appropriate in this case.

Again, getting the balance right is important and any reference to D474 operational level activity will generate interest from others. It is important to ensure the technology or tools selected are fully supported by the organization at all levels.

What is the intended outcome? Here, you should be able to describe the result and benefit of these actions for D474. This principle is clear in describing the scene for an intended outcome. The result is the successful delivery of accurate and confident data for D474. The finalized data principle now reads as follows:

> Use of technology and tools to maintain highest standards of quality (use of data analytics, cleansing and profiling) to deliver accurate and confident data for D474.

The next D474 data principle focuses on data policy making. The draft reads as follows:

> Policy-making function which will oversee legal, handling and security requirements over data use, extraction, sharing, and acquirement.

What is the principle? Here, it is important to think about a specific issue or title. This principle is all about the creation of a D474 policy function. What does a policy-making function entail? Although there is no specific definition here, the principle does go on to explain its scope of responsibility. Perhaps this can be amended as follows:

> A data policy function which will support data-related issues including legal, regulation and compliance, handling and security requirements over data use, extraction, sharing and acquirement.

Now the principle expressly states that D474 policy function is related to data. It also includes the subject areas of regulation and compliance. These, of course, are closely related to legal, but it is important to capture these areas because they form integral parts of the D474 data governance structure.

Why is this principle a potential problem? Here, you should be thinking about summarizing the concern, concept, or issue. D474 questions may arise about the principle and its remit. The principle mentions several issues each of which is a large, complex area. Will a D474 centralized function be able to cover all these issues sufficiently and with due diligence? Or, is this crossing into other areas of the business that already have acquired this specialism or expertise? It is worth testing these draft principles with those D474 stakeholders likely to be affected by these changes. To mitigate the risk of D474 stakeholders effectively *pushing back* against this proposal, it might be worth considering amending the principle as follows:

> A data policy function which will support data-related issues including *working collaboratively with the business in* legal, regulation and compliance, handling and security requirements over data use, extraction, sharing, and acquirement.

Amending the principle in this way ensures that there is enough scope to bring in expertise from other parts of the D474 business.

How will you address the issue? Here, the principle should be able to summarize the process or activity undertaken to resolve or mitigate. Although working collaboratively helps to reassure other business areas of D474, the underlying issue of ownership and accountability remains. However, the principle is effectively setting the tone for a future way of working. As D474 programmes and groups start to work together on individual projects, the details of remit, scope, and accountabilities can be established at the time. Having this flexibility ensures D474 teams within the central function can get the balance right, which is important in helping to establish a good working relationship with key stakeholders.

The next step to consider is *what is the intended outcome?* Here, you should be able to describe the result and benefit of these actions.

The statement is implicit in the assumption that a D474 centralized function will benefit the organization. Having a central point of control helps the organization in terms of managing policies, processes, and checks. Ensuring there is one place to handle, mitigate, or resolve data-related matters prevents roles and responsibilities from being duplicated elsewhere. It may be worth making the D474 centralized role more explicit here. For example:

> On behalf of *D474, a new centralized* data policy function will support data-related issues including *working collaboratively with the business in* legal, regulation, and compliance, handling and security requirements over data use, extraction, sharing, and acquirement.

Setting out the strategic picture can clarify it and help the D474 audience understand the intended outcome for data policy. Putting the principle into context with significant business change allows the reader to understand how this statement supports the wider view.

Finally, let's review the last principle using the same method:

> Produce relevant guidance and raising business awareness related to data responsibilities and accountabilities.

1. What is the principle? Here, it is important to think about a specific issue or title. The principle focuses on producing guidance and raising awareness on matters related to D474 data responsibilities and accountability. This is pitched appropriately at a high level to capture both broad yet important subjects – or is it?

2. Why is this principle a potential problem? Here, you should be thinking about summarizing the concern, concept, or issue. Although this principle is stated in abstract terms, does it really help the D474 audience understand the issue at hand?

One could argue there is a difference between D474 responsibility and accountability. On the other hand, they could be part of the same thing. Obviously both accountability and responsibility are closely related but there are nuanced differences between the two. With regards to accountability, this is really about *whom* in D474 is ultimately the final decision maker. Within an organization such as D474, this is likely to be a senior manager or a member of the executive board. By comparison, smaller businesses are likely to merge data governance into a broader management role. For example, given the potentially smaller scope of activity and resource available, it is more to do with necessity. Think economics of scale and the approach makes more sense. Returning to the principle in hand, is there a clear understanding of D474 responsibility and accountability? Is the distinction brought out clearly enough in the principle?

> Produce relevant guidance and raising business awareness related to data — *in particular,* responsibilities and accountabilities.

The inclusion of "in particular" draws the D474 audience towards responsibilities and accountabilities as two separate and distinct entities. The term "in particular" could be challenged. Is it strong enough as a term to make readers understand the objective? Others may appreciate the nuance and given this is a high-level principle, it may be acceptable to cover this subject matter for now.

3. How will you address the issue? The principle should be able to summarize the D474 process or activity undertaken to resolve or mitigate. The purpose of this question is to clarify or remove any grey areas. Therefore, being more explicit about the role of governance in this subject matter will help the D474 audience understand why it is an important matter to raise. Because of potential ambiguity, there is a need to drill down into the detail and deliver further clarity. The principle has now been amended:

> Produce relevant guidance and raising business awareness related to data — *in particular, supporting governance over* responsibilities and accountabilities.

The amendments now address the potential issue of ambiguity and show *how* the principle will support a wider function of governance. But to what end? This brings us to the final question:

4. What is the intended outcome? Here, you should be able to describe the result and benefit of these actions.

It is anticipated that having a form of governance to support D474 decision-makers will be useful. Any guidance produced to navigate across grey areas will also help the business. We know that D474 lines between responsibility and accountability can be potentially blurred. However, through the delivery of effective guidance and governance, there is a clearer pathway for running an efficient service for the business.

> Produce relevant guidance and raise D474 business awareness related to data — *in particular, supporting governance over* responsibilities and accountabilities — *to deliver better quality service.*

From the examples above, you can see that the data principles are high-level and somewhat abstract. The reason for this is simple; principles should be written broadly enough to encompass all potential aspects of the data strategy. The finalized data principles for D474 are set out below.

D474 Data Principle	Comments
Capture, store, retain, and manage data *using relevant technology for* the benefit of D474 as an organization.	Amended to define scope for data across all the D474 enterprise.
Use of technology and tools to maintain highest standards of quality (use of data analytics, cleansing and profiling) to deliver accurate and confident data for D474.	Important to state the organization is progressive and the technology or tools selected are fully supported at all levels.
On behalf of D474, a new centralized data policy function will support data-related issues including working collaboratively with the business in legal, regulation, and compliance, handling and security requirements over data use, extraction, sharing, and acquirement.	Amended to explicitly show data governance is being managed centrally by a new function, on behalf of the organization.
Produce relevant guidance and raise D474 business awareness related to data - *in particular, supporting governance over* responsibilities and accountabilities - *to deliver better quality service.*	Amended to clarify scope and meaning of data for greater understanding across the organization.

We have now looked at D474 as a fictional test case to illustrate what issues may feature when deciding to implement a system of data governance. The above is to merely illustrate what issues and steps an organization might face when implementing data governance. In some ways, data governance is not a one size fits all t-shirt. Rather, it is a bespoke, tailored fitting. It is important to take the relevant data governance materials that best apply to your organization and weave them into existing practices. Taking a pragmatic and practical approach will help to ensure that any new data governance will take effect and have a positive impact.

Conclusion

One main theme of this book has been to consider the proposition to introduce data governance into mainstream business awareness. To achieve this goal requires adopting a sales or marketing-like pitch to promote the benefits of improved data to assist critical management decisions. To achieve this requires a clear data strategy that sets out the direction and ambition for the organization.

Once the strategic vision has been captured and articulated by the organization, the next phase is to move towards realizing a data governance function. As set out above, establishing effective data governance requires a clear understanding of the current business and its practices. It is more about taking a holistic view of your business and starting with assets that have no physical nature such as company trademarks, patents, goodwill, and software to include. The capture, storage and movement of data underpin all functional aspects of an organization.

If an organization is willing to take steps to implement a data governance function, it must understand the current state of its IT systems and how they manage data. One of the first things that any business or organization must do is work out the value of its data. Data value is not just a case of attributing figures to a dataset. Or exploiting new revenue stream opportunities through company big data.

As with most things the fluidity of data is such that some things that have been captured may quickly become redundant. This is where establishing a foundation of good data governance comes into its own. In terms of implementing data governance in a practical way, here are the key points:

- Use standardized processes that every part of the organization can use.
- Understand your audience to avoid any ambiguities.
- Keep things simple.
- Warm up your stakeholders in advance by bringing them in early and raising awareness at any given opportunity.
- Anticipate challenges in advance by testing issues beforehand to ensure you are prepared for a variety of outcomes.

So, what does the future hold for data governance?

We have seen data governance evolve from a technically driven set of rules to meet data standards, to a broader system of regulation and controls across data quality, security, and now data privacy.

Data governance is playing catch up with technology developments. One way of applying controls on technology is the use of legislation such as the GDPR to ensure the organization manages data effectively and ethically.

Organizations have shared data in the background for some time. Sasha Molitorisz's article brings to light the business of data sharing. Otherwise known as data brokers, these companies facilitate the use of personal identifiable information which can be used by advertising companies for a price.[41] Data brokering is a legitimate and lucrative activity. However, the fact that it has been happening in the background without enough regulation is potentially a cause for concern for data privacy. It may take some time for regulators to ensure sufficient controls are in place. But in the meantime, data governance has emerged as an effective mechanism to both raise awareness and to regulate the use of personalized data. By introducing data governance systems to companies, the ability to apply standards and track transactions at any given stage provides the opportunity for organizations to stay in control of their data management.

---

[41] It's time for third-party data brokers to emerge from the shadows; Molitorisz, S; The Conversation.com https://bit.ly/2QkegXj (accessed 23/06/18).

With established technology-disrupting industries such as banking and healthcare, it will become more important for organizations to self-regulate the management of their data assets. In the near future, Sam Mitha suggests data could be the key to modernizing taxation across disruptive technologies.[42]

In banking, the number of financial technology companies otherwise known as 'fintech' continue to rise as they look to harness technologies such as blockchain to provide secure yet alternative banking facilities like electronic peer to peer lending for example. Regulation in this space again will be playing catch up as new technologies emerge to disrupt the status quo. However, the UK government has recognized the potential of fintech start-ups and is working together with regulators and the financial industry to further explore these opportunities.[43]

Technologies like the Internet of Things (IoT), which effectively allow the connection of different devices to share data, will need to have some form of security to protect user information. Perhaps the growing popularity of personalized cloud space offered by the likes of Amazon, Google, and Microsoft will require further scrutiny in how information is stored and used.

---

[42] Mitha, S; Robots, Technological Change and Taxation; Tax Journal; https://bit.ly/2RFaLri (accessed 28/05/18).

[43] Fintech Sector Strategy; Policy Paper; HM Treasury; 22/03/18 https://bit.ly/2pw1DZN (accessed 23/06/18).

We can see that artificial intelligence is continuing to develop at a pace alongside technology for automated vehicles. With all this disruption emerging within the technology industry, the need for applying a form of control is essential. Legislation will continue to be on the back foot as it is reactionary by its nature. In other words, the legislative process takes time as it passes through the legal process to become enshrined in law. There is a gap in the process and this is where data governance comes into its own.

Data governance provides organizations with the opportunity to self-regulate and manage data transactions effectively and efficiently. Having a centralized set of data standards and controls help companies become more transparent with data management and comply with more stringent legislation. Data governance is more than just a set of technical standards, it is a practical way for organizations to get on the front foot and understand the value of data. Data governance will continue to evolve alongside technology as both areas expand in the future.

In summary, data governance is here to stay and will continue to evolve as a function. The fluidity of data governance will help to grow its role both as an enforcer of legislation and an embracer of new technologies.

Bibliography

A Brief Introduction to China's Cybersecurity Law; China Law Insight; (accessed 31 August 2017) https://bit.ly/2B5xKoo.

A new data leak hits Aadhaar, India's national ID database; Whittaker, Zack; for Zero Day on ZDnet; https://zd.net/2JETbP5 (accessed 23/03/18).

Artificial Intelligence: The Basics; Warwick, K; Routledge; 2013.

Big Data Governance: An Emerging Imperative; Soares, S; MC Press, LLC; 2012.

Blockchain Technology: Introduction to Blockchain Technology and its impact on Business Ecosystem; Fleming, S; Stephen Fleming; 2017.

Business Architecture: The Art and Practice of Business Transformation; Ulrich, W; McWhorter, N; Meghan-Kiffer Press, 2010.

The Business Blockchain: Promise, Practice, and Application of the Next Internet Technology; Mougayar, W; John Wiley & Sons; 2016.

China's Cybersecurity Law gives the Ministry of State Security unprecedented powers over foreign technology (accessed 31 August 2017) https://bit.ly/2Ep2x3g.

The Cult of Information: A Neo-Luddite Treatise on High Tech, Artificial Intelligence and the True Art of Thinking; Roszak, T; Berkeley, University of California Press; 1994.

Data Governance: High-impact Strategies – What You Need to Know: Definitions, Adoptions, Impact, Benefits, Maturity, Vendors; Roebuck K; Lightning Source; 2011.

Data Governance: How to Design, Deploy and Sustain an Effective Data Governance Program; Ladley, J; Newnes; 2012.

Data Modelling for MongoDB: Building Well-Designed and Supportable MongoDB Databases; Hoberman, S; Technics Publications, 2014.

Data Simplification: Taming information with open source tools; Berman, Jules J. (Morgan Kaufmann) 2016.

Effective Master Data Management with SAP NetWeaver MDM; Walker A; Ganapathy, J; Galileo Press; 2008.

Enterprise Data Governance: Reference and Master Data Management Semantic Modelling; Bonnet, P; John Wiley and Sons; 2013.

Enterprise Architecture As Strategy: Creating a Foundation for Business Execution; Ross, J.W.; Weill, P; Robertson, D; Harvard Business Press; 2006.

The Essential Writings of Machiavelli; Machiavelli, N; Edited by Constantine, P; Modern Library, 2007.

Exploring Corporate Strategy; Johnson, G; Scholes, K; Whittington, R; Financial Times; Prentice Hall; 2010.

Factsheet: What is the role of the Board? Institute of Directors https://bit.ly/2krGta8 (Accessed 28/02/18).

Globalization and Governance; Hart, J.A.; Prakash, A; Routledge; 2003.

Governance, Globalization and Public Policy; Kennett, P; Edward Elgar Publishing; 2008.

Governance Structures and Mechanisms in Public Service Organizations: Theories, Evidence and Future Directions; Calabro, A; Springer Science & Business Media; 2011.

Information Governance: Concepts, Strategies, and Best Practices; Smallwood, R.F; John Wiley & Sons; 2014.

Introduction to Artificial Intelligence: Second, Enlarged Edition; Jackson, P.C.; Courier Corporation; 2013.

IT Governance: An International Guide to Data Security and ISO27001/ISO27002; Calder, A; Watkins, S; Kogan Page Publishers; 2015.

Master Data Management and Data Governance, 2/E; Berson, A; Dubov; L, McGraw Hill Professional; 2010.

Non-Invasive Data Governance: The Path of Least Resistance and Greatest Success; Seiner, R.S; Technics Publications; 2014.

The Practical Adoption of Agile Methodologies; The Association for Project Management, APM North West; 2015.

Reassembling the social: An introduction to actor-network-theory; Latour, B.; Oxford University Press; 2005.

Rebels Against the Future: The Luddites and Their War on the Industrial Revolution: Lessons for the Computer Age; Sale, K.; Massachusetts Addison-Wesley; 1995.

USGS Data Management Data Stewardship: Roles and Responsibilities. https://bit.ly/2Gaj39j (accessed 15/10/17).

The visual imperative: creating a visual culture of data discovery; Ryan, Lindy; Morgan Kaufmann; 2016.

What is Data Ethics; Luciano, F; Taddao, M; Philosophical Transactions of the Royal Society https://bit.ly/2tSL9uS (Accessed 17/12/17).

Lightning Source UK Ltd.
Milton Keynes UK
UKHW021203210122
397522UK00008B/1829